Praying on Purpose

Intentional Growth through Prayer

Eric L. Leake

www.xulonpress.com

CONTENTS

—⟨∞⟩—

Section Four: The Power of Prayer

DEDICATION

In Memory of

My dear grandmother, Willia Mae Chambers Haywood
Dumas, who taught me the power of prayer.

Breck Ellison, Jr.,
who taught so many of us how to pray
in the midst of pain, pressures, and problems.
He prayed for and loved pastors unto the end.

Louise Scott, Dora Wilson, and Barbara Jean Porter,
prayer warriors who all went home to be
with the Lord in 2012.
their commitment to prayer blessed so many of us, even
now many prayers that they prayed are being answered.
We will long remember these praying women!

In Honor of our parents

Eugene and Pearl McMurray

Sarah Jean Dumas Leake

and William Richard Johnson

and

Those who constantly pray for my family, the ministry,

and me. They are too numerous to name!

Thank you for your prayers, they are making a

difference. May God bless and keep you all.

ACKNOWLEDGMENTS

———∞∞∞———

$\mathcal{I}$ want to first thank God for giving me the wisdom, strength, courage, and provisions to write this book on prayer.

To my wife Jean for her assistance, contribution, prayers, and tenacity through this journey.

To our children, Jessica, Joshua, Caleb, and Elijah for allowing me the time to make this writing possible. I want to thank our grandson, Jeremiah, who would often come to the study and just ask, "Papaw, are you all right?" I'm grateful for your love and respect for me.

To the Greater Warner Tabernacle A.M.E. Zion Church, Knoxville, Tennessee, for allowing me to unfold my prayer journey and assignment with them twenty years ago. We learned to pray and fast together to get through the tough times.

To the Martin Temple A.M.E. Zion Church, Chicago, Illinois, for giving me the time and space to complete this assignment and for embracing the ministry of prayer as we continue the journey. To the Ministerial Staff for their willingness to partner with and assist me in ministry so that ministry assignments like this could be completed. I'm amazed at your commitment and grateful to God for your continued servant hood. To Mr. Roy Tolbert for Graphic design at the beginning of each chapter.

I am thankful to several friends who would ask me from time to time, "How is the book coming?" It was an encouragement to get to this point. Those persons were my secretary, Debbie Stokes; my prayer partners, James R. Bridgeman, Jason Perry, and Tony Collins; Rev. Mamie Cooper, who would always ask me, "Have you done what the Lord told you to do yet?" and others like Teresa Oglesby and my sister, Benita McGuine, who would remind me of the importance of sharing what God has placed inside of me to bring it forth to share with others. I'm grateful for those who proofread and edited and made critical and constructive comments about this writing.

To those who read this writing and penned an endorsement in the midst of your own ministry assignments, I am eternally grateful. Thank you all for your contributions to my life and ministry. To God be the glory for each of you!

THE FOREWORD

Bishop Darryl B. Starnes, Sr.

From the very first time that I met Eric Leake, I knew that there was something special about him. I was a young pastor in the African Methodist Episcopal Zion Church, and he was a teenager and the chaplain of the Varick Christian Youth Council of the denomination. His spirituality was so authentic and his leadership was so strong that four years later he was elected the President of this national organization. When he entered the ministry, he immediately became a catalyst for revitalization and growth in the congregations to which he was appointed as pastor. He went on to develop a track record of turning around congregations that were facing some of the most difficult and most challenging circumstances.

For several years, he served as a Presiding Elder, with supervisory responsibilities for the spiritual and temporal well-being of the churches on his district. Dr. Eric Leake was also an invaluable resource for the Bureau of Evangelism of the denomination during the twelve years that I served as its director. For decades, he has been in great demand throughout the country as a convention speaker and seminar facilitator on the subject of Church Revitalization. Of great significance is the fact that he has been a catalyst for bringing pastors and city leaders together for unified prayer that has brought lasting change to the community.

Dr. Leake's dynamic prayer life has been the secret of his success as a young leader, a pastor, a Presiding Elder, a community leader, and a denominational leader. Now, it is my privilege to serve as his bishop. I am compelled to report that his leadership as the Prayer Coordinator of the Episcopal District is a major reason for the transformation that God is bringing about in the Episcopal area.

In the endeavors that really matter in life, a skilled, capable, and experienced coach makes all the difference. A coach makes a difference not only in the performance of each player, but more importantly, in the performance of the team. Dr. Eric Leake is a skilled player-coach in the ministry of prayer. He has been a series student of prayer for more than two decades. More importantly, he has been a serious practitioner of prayer for more than four decades. Through his example of prayer and his teachings on prayer, he has helped many believers to reach their full potential as disciples of Christ. He has coached many pastors in the dynamics of prayer ministry; and he has led congregations in overcoming great obstacles to make a positive and lasting difference in their communities.

Our generation and those that follow will benefit greatly from the fact that Dr. Leake has chosen to capture his vast knowledge, deep insights, and unique perspectives on prayer in this practical, easy-to-read book. In *Praying on Purpose*, Dr. Leake does not simply give theories on prayer; he enters into the trenches of life with us, and he literally coaches us in the nuts and bolts of practical, real-life, prevailing prayer. He clarifies the relationship between our quality time with God and our spiritual growth and character development. He not only convinces us of the necessity of being intentional about prayer, he also explains the far-reaching benefits of praying on purpose.

This well-written volume will become a timeless resource for God's people. Through it laypersons can be helped in developing the discipline to pray purposefully, grow spiritually, and be equipped in effective prayer ministry. Pastors will find help and hope as they grapple with the challenges of leading churches in need of revitalization. Furthermore, congregations that are struggling can be turned around through these practical prayer principles and eventually can be transformed into dynamic, disciple-making entities.

Darryl B. Starnes, Sr., Bishop, Midwest Episcopal Area

African Methodist Episcopal Zion Church, Charlotte, North Carolina

CHAPTER ONE

THE PRINCIPLES OF PRAYER

———⟨∕∕∕⟩———

*T*he Lord Jesus Christ calls us to come, follow and serve Him! (Matthew 4:19). This is a call to His kingdom, through discipleship and relationship. There is a duality to our discipleship! It is a call to walk and talk with Jesus and like Jesus! In order for this to be lived out in our lives, we must become intentional Christian disciples. A Christian disciple is a student of Jesus Christ, one who follows his teachings and His will. Discipleship is one becoming passionate about one's relationship with Jesus Christ and is intentional about growing to Christian maturity.

While there should be noticeable growth in the life of a Christian, questions being asked are "what does growth look like," "how can others know if a Christian is experiencing transformation," and "how does an individual know if they are moving toward Christian maturity?" According to Neil Anderson and Robert Saucy in their book *Unleashing God's Power in You*, "As believers, we should be progressing, growing able to say, "'I am more loving, more peaceful, more patient, (and so on) than I was last year, and I am falling more in love with God and others every day.' If we can't say that, then we are not growing, and we are missing out on life."[1] Each person should engage in a consistent spiritual growth plan that will enhance their Christian journey. The health of a Christian can be observed through Paul's writings in Galatians 5: 22-23: "But the fruit of the Spirit is love, joy, peace, longsuffering, gentleness, goodness, faith, meekness, temperance: against such there is no law" (KJV). These spiritual attributes should be expressed through the life of a mature Christian disciple. However, a concern for many American Christians is that people within the Movement are not reaching the full maturity of the Lord Jesus Christ (Ephesians 4:13). For example, too often Christians grow in ministry but not in spirituality. Gifts and talents are often developed, while Christian character is neglected. While many opportunities

---

[1] Neil Anderson and Robert Saucy, *Unleashing God's Power in You* (Eugene, Oregon: Harvest House Publishers, 2004). 12.

are offered for growth and nurturing, there seem to be only a few individuals who have a passion to grow, take advantage of growth opportunities, and learn as disciples. In order for this type of transformation to occur, those who faithfully follow Jesus are challenged to do more than believe: to grow in their Christian faith. Being a disciple of Christ is more than a theoretical concept: it is a practical lifestyle, which is seen through the Christian's behavior. It often appears that many who signed up for the Christian journey have become spiritual dropouts for one reason or another, but growing spiritually should never be an option, but an intentional endeavor to become a mature Christian disciple.

One spiritual discipline to aid in the development of a Christian disciple is prayer. John Wesley, the founder of the Methodist Church, regarded prayer as the chief discipline or "means of grace." Prayer keeps the disciple in touch with Christ. Prayer can also be used as an agent of change and character development. Can people grow spiritually through prayer? Can Christian disciples learn to practice prayer at every turn in their lives? Can we use prayer as a tool for Christian growth and nurturing? Being disciplined in prayer teaches us to practice prayer even when we do not feel like it. Just as we need physical disciplines to get and stay in shape physically, we need spiritual discipline to spiritually stay in shape. We must be diligent, dutiful, and dedicated to growing up in Christ through the means of prayer. E.M. Bounds notes the importance of prayer in the shaping of the Christian's character:

> Prayer governs conduct, and conduct makes character.
> Conduct is what we do. Character is what we are. Character
> is the root of the tree. Conduct is the fruit it bears. Prayer
> is related to all gifts of grace. Prayer helps to establish
> character and fashion conduct. Prayer helps where all
> other aids fail. The more we pray, the better we are, and
> the purer and better our lives become.[2]

Prayer has been the foundation and subject for numerous people for centuries. There have been great debates about prayer, like whether it should be done in private or in public and whether prayer is effective or ineffective. Yet, there are many who have come to realize that prayer is more precious than money, fame, or education. For those who have come through great difficulties, they will exclaim, "I prayed my way through!" Prayer is the Christian's weapon for coping with the warfare and welfare of life. Look around and one will discover that those who trust God,

---

[2] E.M. Bounds, *E.M. Bounds on Prayer* (New Kensington, PA: Whitaker House, 1997), 148.

walk with Him, and enjoy a mutual relationship and experience victorious Christian living; are people who pray.

While prayer is a powerful and simple act, it is often the most neglected in the life of many Christian believers. Because we are not born praying, prayer must become a learned attribute for those who seek God's face, guidance, and the moving of His hand. If prayer is to be effective, Christians must pursue such a habit with diligence. I believe it is the Lord's desire that every Christian disciple become a habitual prayer warrior. Therefore, we must learn to pray and how to pray.

Perhaps this could be the reason one disciple asked Jesus in Luke 11, to "teach us to pray . . ." (KJV). The key is not that we know how to pray as much as we know to pray. Prayer helps us find the way. Talking to God, listening, and waiting for His response prove over and over again that praying on purpose is God's way for the Christian disciple. Through prayer we victoriously make our way through challenges, conflicts, changes, temptations, tribulations, tests, trials, pressures, pains, persecutions, and the problems we encounter daily. We are also able to enjoy the benefit of prayer during seasons of encouragement, renewal, and revival in our own lives.

Prayer should always be the first and last order of business on the agenda for the Christian because it keeps us connected with God. Prayer is the key to an effective walk with God, a thriving ministry, an ordered life, strong family ties, and a positive Christian influence within the communities where we are being called to shape, serve, and share.

So, why write another book on prayer, some may ask, because there are numerous resources already written and taught on prayer. Each individual is inspired by the Holy Spirit in different ways according to culture, experience, and direction. I have a burning desire to coach people into becoming people of prayer and to grow spiritually in the process. I am compelled to coach people in praying through every season, situation, and struggle in their lives. On numerous occasions I have inquired of people about their struggles and would ask, "Have you prayed about it?"

Many would often respond, "I have been praying, but it's not working," or "I don't know how to pray," and for others, "I have prayed, but I don't know what else to do." These statements influenced this writing in huge ways. Engaging people in prayer on a regular basis—from my own personal experience—can be a great challenge. As a result, this book was born because of God's people who desire and need help with their prayer journey.

This book has been written to encourage, equip, and empower people in prayer and to utilize prayer as a means for spiritual growth and nurturing. It is designed to assist people in understanding the purpose, power, presence, peace, practice, and provisions of prayer in times like these. The hope is to help people become more intentional about their relationship with the Lord Jesus Christ through the discipline of prayer. Praying on purpose implies that one is intentional about praying and growing. It says, "I mean to do this." Praying on purpose is not something one does by accident or coincidence but with a plan and purpose in mind. If Christians are intentional about singing, preaching, teaching, serving, working, shopping, and other habits, why can't we develop the habit of praying on purpose and be intentional about our Christian maturity?

Several methods of prayer are discussed to direct you to pray specific kinds of prayers for specific needs and circumstances. The title of this book could easily be *Praying Through* because it teaches us to pray at every turn of life. The chapters of this writing introduce us to the purpose of prayer and encourage us to pray the scriptures. They also guide us in understanding the importance of praying in times like these. Prayer topics have been designed for growth through learning about the prayer life of Jesus, and praying disciples. In addition, you will find the practice of prayer through adoration, confession, supplication, and intercession. The power of prayer is offered through fasting, thanksgiving, and how God answers ours prayers. Prayers and study questions follow at the end of each chapter, and these resources can be used privately or in a small group setting. Hopefully you will find spiritual insight, information, and inspiration from this guide to prayer. May you grow in the grace and knowledge of the Lord Jesus Christ through a strong and consistent prayer life as you pray on purpose!

CHAPTER TWO

IT'S PRAYING TIME!

This chapter addresses the signs of the age and the season of life we are in. Although these are times of great educational, technological, and medical advancement, these are also times of great sin, selfishness, sorrow, sadness, doubt, depression, distractions, disease, despair, discouragement, and disappointments. The people of God are being attacked on all fronts. Emotional sickness is just as rampart as physical illness. Drugs, sex, and immorality are plaguing our society like never before. It's a time when neither Jesus Christ nor His Christians are popular, especially when we stand and fight for what pleases Him. This leads me to one conclusion, its praying time! It's time for us to bombard heaven and shake hell with the power of prayer. If the saints don't pray who will? If Christians neglect prayer, then who will talk to God and who will listen to God? Yes, it is evident from the signs of the times in the news and in our cities that it's high time for the people of God to pray.

The times we live in are difficult times, and they try our very souls, patience, and often test our walk with God. If we are to break the strongholds, true Christian disciples must go back to being people of prayer. While there is a lot of work to do, the work must be reinforced with prayer. If we are intentional about preaching, teaching, singing, working, serving, bathing, eating, sleeping, and dressing, then let us rise up and be intentional about praying because it is praying time! It appears that while we are more educated, we have less wisdom, more technology and less tolerance, more money but less time for God and family. Thus comes the reminder that it's praying time!

We do not always pray because we ought to; we pray because we need to. Prayer helps us keep our sanity in insane times, brings the presence of God into any situation, offers peace in the midst of confusion, provides joy in the midst of sorrow, and gives direction in dark and devastating times. Yes, it's praying time. We must not just pray with our lips, but also with our minds, hearts, and spirit.

If we are going to advance to the Kingdom of God, prayer is the channel by which it will be done!

We must pray like never before. While we pray to stay in touch with the Lord, we must also pray, to be able to stand against the attacks of the enemy. It's praying time because it's fighting time! When it comes to dealing with spiritual warfare, prayer is at the center of the battle. As the Apostle Paul writes about putting on the whole armor of God, he finally commends to us the ministry and practice of prayer. Because of the intense times that we are living in, to learn to fight the good fight of faith is to learn to pray and do it effectively. For the Christian, prayer must be more than a routine, ritualistic, or religious act—it must be a force that drives out the works of darkness from around us and ushers in the presence of God!

Prayer will work when nothing else will. Prayer will help when money, materials goods, and human-made gimmicks will not. If prayer won't help, what will? If we are going to be "more than conquerors" and win every battle fought, have every habit broken, every problem solved, every hurdle crossed, and every issue resolved, it must be through strategic prayer. We cannot fight in our own strength, intellect, and power. In must be in the Lord's strength and in the Lord's might. When we fight in the Lord's might, we realize that the Lord is strong and mighty because He's all knowing, all seeing, and all powerful! So let's establish that the battle is not in our strength, but in the Lord's strength. This means that if we are going to fight, we must depend upon the Lord more than we depend upon ourselves. Praying teaches us that God is in control, not us. We can often lose strength and faint on the way, but the Lord never loses strength. The greatest power for the Christian in warfare is praying power.

The battles raging around us are fierce, sharp, subtle, and sudden. Therefore we must be able to stand against the wiles of the devil: his schemes, plots, and strategies. Unless we know who the enemy is, what the enemy can do, where the enemy is, and who the enemy can use, we will have a hard time defeating the enemy. We do not fight for victory; we fight because Jesus Christ has already given us the victory and the authority to fight. We fight because Satan comes to steal, kill, and destroy.

Prayer is just as much a part of spiritual warfare as the armor itself. To put on the armor and not pray is to have no armor on at all. The battle is not a physical battle; it is a spiritual battle. It's a battle that you cannot see with the naked eye. Therefore, you cannot fight this battle in the natural because there are unseen evil forces all around us. We do not fight against flesh and blood.

In Ephesians 6:10, we are directed to put on the whole armor of God. We are to be fully armed and dressed for the battle. How we dress determines how we persevere in the battle. However, after we get dressed up, then it is time to pray up. We discover that truth and prayer go together, while righteousness and prayer go together as well. If one would have peace, there must be prayer close by. If our faith is to be strong, then our prayers must be strong. Likewise, prayer and salvation go together and surely the word of God and prayer are matches for life and ministry. This implies that whatever we are called to do, we are serving on one hand, while praying on the other. In the following section, we are admonished to pray in a certain manner in praying times.

Pray Always

Praying always implies that we must pray without ceasing. People always wonder if you have to stop everything you're doing to pray. Sometimes it's good, but all the time you can't. Sometimes we have to work and pray, drive and pray, or serve and pray. Praying always teaches us that we must always be in communion with God. When we are talking to people on the telephone and the conversation is over, we usually hang up the phone unless there is another call. However, "praying always" teaches us to never ever hang up the phone on God. Keep the phone off the hook and stay connected with God. Whatever we are called to do, prayer should always be the force that moves us along. Hence, we are commanded to pray always. Not sometimes, but all the time. This teaches us to live a lifestyle of prayer and to remain in a prayerful mood at all times. It's like preaching and praying, teaching and praying, singing and praying, leading and praying, or pastoring and praying. When we learn to "pray always" we learn to pray privately, publicly, openly, silently, walking, running, standing, kneeling, lying, and so forth. This helps us to live out Luke 18:1, "to always pray and not to faint" (KJV). I Thessalonians 5:17 directs us to "pray without ceasing" (KJV). The intent here is to be in prayer at every point of life. This helps us to become prayer-directed or prayer-propelled saints.

Pray Different Ways

Paul also writes about praying "with all prayer" because there are many ways to pray. When I was growing up, I thought prayer was only about making a wish list and checking things off as God answered. While there is a time for that kind of prayer, that's not the only way to pray. We must learn that in the heat of the battle, there is more than one way to pray. The Lord has provided ways to pray at every turn in life and for every situation. These diverse ways of praying will be discussed and demonstrated in the next section of the book on "The Practice of Prayer."

Pray In the Spirit

Paul notes that when we pray we should not only pray always, pray different ways, but also to pray in the spirit. There is great discussion about what it means to pray in the spirit, but whatever kind of way we pray, it must fit the situation, and it must be in the spirit. In other words, there is a difference between saying prayers and praying. Praying in the spirit is praying in the will of God. We can pray long, we can pray loud, and we can pray hard, but if the Holy Spirit is not in it, we have not effectively prayed. We can say prayers and they will never reach the throne room without the spirit of God. Romans 8:26-27 teaches us that "we don't know how to pray as we ought" (KJV), but the Holy Spirit prays through us, with us, and sometimes for us. We must be mindful that however we pray, whether it is in tongues or in our native language, it must be in the Spirit. Our prayers ought to be Holy Spirit led, Holy Spirit directed, and Holy Spirit controlled. "The prayers of the righteous availeth much" (James 5:16, KJV). We should pray with power, passion, and purpose, all of which

29

are Holy Spirit driven. When this happens, then we can truly acknowledge that we have prayed in the Spirit. Praying in the spirit yields results that otherwise cannot be found praying in the flesh. It is the Holy Spirit that gives life to our prayers.

Pray and Watch

The Apostle Paul admonishes those who pray, to pray while watching thereunto. This implies watchfulness, being alert, and discerning the times and seasons around us. Praying and watching helps us to know how to direct our prayers and how things are moving by the Holy Spirit of God. Not only have we been encouraged to pray, but we are also encouraged to watch and pray. We must be alert! Watching and praying reminds us *to* "be careful! Watch out for attacks from the devil, your great enemy. He prowls around like a roaring lion, looking for some victim to devour" (1 Peter 5:8 NLT). We must watch because we never know which way the enemy is coming. So in battle you need to be alert. Prayer alone will not hold back the enemy. Henceforth, we must be aware of his tactics, devices, plots, and schemes. This means that we must be careful and prayerful watchers at the same time. This calls for diligence in our prayer life and being intentional in discerning what's taking place around us. Some people call this type of prayer "praying with your eyes open." Jesus Christ told His disciples in the Garden of Gethsemane in Matthew 26:41, "Watch and pray that ye enter not into temptation" (KJV). As the Lord directs and we obey, we are better prepared for prayer. If we are not wise, we could easily watch without praying and be devoured by the enemy. However, we could be praying without watching, refusing to heed the voice of God, and be attacked suddenly as well. Watching and praying go together in times of warfare and intense battle. This area of praying helps us to be more sensitive and intelligent in how we should pray. It keeps us from being ignorant in our prayer lives but allows us to trust the Holy Spirit more to lead us in our praying.

Pray with Perseverance

Perseverance is important in this battle because this is a tough fight and sometimes it's a difficult battle; we sometimes get wounded in the fight, and we get weary from fighting and want to quit. However, we must never give up in the midst of the battle. We cannot afford to be passive in this fight. The Kingdom of God cannot be advanced with complaining, complacent, compromising, or comfortable spirits. Therefore, we must be intentional about fighting and our intention to fight will be evident in our persevering in prayer. If you are in the fight, we must be in the fight for the long haul. One of the greatest awakenings that I ever had is that the Christian journey is not a sprint, but a marathon! It's no secret that we now live in a quick-fix, microwave, ATM, drive-through, society. We don't want to wait, work, or fight for anything for a long period of time. But we must to able to stand firm in the midst of adversity, stand firm when all hell breaks loose, and stand firm in the hope of the Lord Jesus Christ. Perseverance is important in the battle because if we are in the fight, we must be in the fight for the long haul. If we are going to pray, we must learn the power of steadfast endurance. We must stay steady under the load. When things get difficult and we see no end, deliverance, or results in sight, we must press on in prayer. Too often we quit praying when things have not changed in a limited amount of time. Persevering in prayer builds our faith and trust in God and not in others or ourselves. I believe learning to wait on God and persevering in prayer teaches us to put our confidence in the Lord and not in the situation that we are facing. Persevering prayer also teaches us to pay attention to what God is doing and saying.

Pray For Others-(Intercession)

Because there is a chapter in this book on intercession, that chapter will reference what we need to know about intercession. However, it is always a blessing to know that others are praying for you. It is likewise a blessing to be able to pray for others. Those who pray for others are blessed as well as those who are prayed for. We are always encouraged in the word of God to pray for one another.

If we are going to be effective in spiritual warfare, prayer must be a high priority. Only prayer warriors can be effective on the frontline of the battlefield. We will never know what it means to fight until we understand what it means to pray, and we will never know what it means to pray until we realize what it means to fight. We must value the significance of prayer because it is praying time. It's praying time, not for a select few, but for everyone. It's praying time in our personal lives; it's praying time in our homes, in our churches, in our communities, and in our cities. Furthermore, it is praying time in our nation and in the world. If life is difficult with prayer, what I want to know is that how do people make it without prayer? Things are often intense while walking with God, although He helps us through each dilemma and guides us through the dangers and snares of life. But for those who refuse to pray or decide to handle life on their own, how will they make it in times like these?

We often speculate, dialogue, and even recommend to people

the discipline of prayer. We can spend more time talking about prayer than we do praying. It's imperative that we are intentional about the Master's business through prayer. We cannot afford to just talk about praying; it's time to pray! God grant us the strength to pray always, with perseverance, in different ways, in the spirit, watching and praying for one another. The saints must be aware of the days that we are living in because prayer is our safety, security, and strength for these days and the days to come. Why? Because it's praying time! If it is praying time, then God's agenda must be at the top of the agenda for every Christian believer.

Perhaps there are many who say they do not know how to pray or for what to pray. Some may even wonder what they need to say. I believe that learning how to pray will come the more we engage in the act of praying. Jesus Christ has provided a way; it is the way to Him, and that way is prayer. May we pray in and out of season because praying time is all the time!

Prayer:

Dear Lord, help me to understand what praying time means and to be an active participant in praying during these trying, challenging, perilous times. Help me to know the power and importance of prayer. I pray Lord that I will pray always, different ways, in the Spirit, watching thereunto, and with perseverance for all the saints. I pray that you would give me the strength to pray even when the battles of life are raging and the spiritual attacks are sharp, intense, and complicated. I ask Lord that I will not be passive or complacent in my prayer life or my prayer time, but that I will press forward daily in the power of prayer and trusting you for the results. I pray that you will help me put on the armor each day so that I might fight the good fight of faith. This I ask in Jesus' Name, Amen!

Study Questions

1. What good do you believe prayer is these days?
2. How has prayer benefited your life?
3. How do prayer and the times we are living in relate to each other?
4. Why is prayer so important in relation to spiritual warfare and handling the attacks of the enemy?
5. How can praying different ways help to improve your prayer life?

Prayer Activity

Spend time praying to put on the Armor of God by using Ephesians 6:10-18. This would include praying and asking God to equip you for the battle and the times that we are living in. Pray for God to equip you with the Armor of Truth (Ephesians 6: 14a), the Armor of Righteousness (Ephesians 6: 14b), the Armor of Peace (Ephesians 6: 15), the Armor of Faith (Ephesians 6:16), the Armor of Salvation (Ephesians 6: 17a), the Armor of Scripture (Ephesians 6: 17b), the Armor of Prayer (Ephesians 6: 18a), and the Armor of Perseverance (Ephesians 6: 18b).

(Suggested use: Pray through these verses for protection, especially during times of heavy warfare and turmoil.)

CHAPTER THREE

PRAYING GOD'S WORD

his chapter is about praying the scriptures. It will discuss the role the Holy Scriptures have in prayer. One of the greatest blessings about praying is that God has given us His word to use as a guide for prayer. In truth, we cannot begin to discuss the purpose, people, practice, and power of prayer without looking at how important the scriptures are in prayer. Praying the scriptures help us to be more purposeful in our praying. Because the word of God is the foundation and authority by which we live, it also serves the same when we pray. If God speaks to us through the Holy Bible, we can also use the Holy Bible to speak to God!

God's word is always relevant because it serves as food for the hungry, water for the thirsty, light for the lost, salvation for the sinners, rest for the weary, a pattern for children, a guide for youth, and comfort for the aged. God's word helps to keep us on the right track because God's word is His voice to us. God's word is a powerful instrument for growth, guidance, deliverance, and our daily walk with the Lord. Isaiah 40:8 informs us that "The grass withers; the flower fades, but the word of God stands forever" (KJV). The word of God for the people of God is just as profound when praying as it is when God speaks to us through His Holy word in meditation, teaching, or preaching! In light of that, it is fitting to engage in prayer with the power and word of God.

Psalm 119 is the base for praying the scriptures because it is prayers about God's word. Psalm 119:105 gives us a clear focus as God's word guides us in prayer. Using God's word to pray and understand God's will is an important aim in this discussion. The purpose for praying the scriptures and practical ways to pray are offered as well. At the end of the chapter are examples of how to pray the scriptures, with hope that these few points will enlighten and mature us as we pray God's word.

In order to understand more clearly prayer and the power of God's word, Psalm 119 gives the setting for praying the scriptures. It also offers prayers to God about His word and about God's agreement with us in His word. It refers to God who acts, speaks, and never breaks His promises. All throughout Psalm 119 are 176 prayers to God about His word, His will, His commandments, and His ways. (Verses 122 and 132 do not refer to His word, but they are prayers as well). Psalm 119 includes purposeful and practical ways to pray the scriptures.

Throughout Psalm 119, we are admonished to read the word, live the word (Psalm 119:1-8), hide the word (Psalm 119:10), know the word (Psalm 119:11), and ponder the word (Psalm 119:15-18). We are also taught to learn the word (Psalm 119: 25-33), understand the word (Psalm 119:34), accept the word (Psalm 119: 65-72), and to trust the word (Psalm 119:81). The Psalmist also instructs us to love the word (Psalm 119:97-104), apply the word (Psalm 119:105), and remember the word (Psalm 119:176). These scriptures in Psalm 119 are reminders of the power, importance, and relevance of God's word in our lives.

Psalm 119:105, reminds us of God's word as a guide for life. Thus the Psalmist notes, "Thy word is a light unto my feet and a light unto my path" (KJV). Therefore, God's word gives us light in dark times and helps us to know where to step, when to step, and how to step. God's word is like a map to a traveler, a recipe to a cook, a blueprint to a carpenter, and a pattern to a seamstress. God's word is our light and our lamp for living. Because the word of God is that powerful in an individual's life, would it not be just as powerful in an individual's *prayer* life? If the word of God guides us in our walk with the Lord, surely it is useful to guide us in our prayer life. If the bible is good for instruction, reproof, rebuke, exhortation, doctrine, and correction, it is also good for prayer. When we pray, God's word is a valuable instrument.

One of the great benefits of praying the scriptures is understanding the will of God. It has been said by some, "When we pray God's word, we pray God's will." God's word reveals God's will and God's ways. For those who struggle with how to pray and understanding the will of God, I suggest you begin with praying the scriptures. We often hear and read about praying in faith and getting what we pray for if our faith is strong enough. However, according to the scriptures, we must always pray in the will of God to be granted that which we are seeking from God. Several scriptures teach us this concept. In Matthew 6 and Luke 11, in what we know as the Lord's prayer records, "Thy Kingdom come, Thy will be done, on earth as it is in heaven." 1 John 5:14-15 notes, "And this is the confidence that we have in Him, that, if we ask any thing according to His will, he heareth us: And if we know that He hears us, whatsoever we ask, we know that we have the petitions that we desired of Him" (KJV). This keeps us from praying our own selfish, personal agenda, "blab it and grab it" kind of prayers. In order to know how to pray, it would then seem to me that our praying must be rooted and grounded in the word of God. When we pray, then praying in the will of God is crucial for the right kind of results. For this reason, if we are not careful, we can pray not only out of selfishness, but out of ignorance. If we are aware of God's word, we are able to pray with intelligence and power. The more we pray God's word, the more in tune we become to God's will.

Praying the scriptures can also help us stay focused when praying. It keeps us from wondering and rambling when we are praying. Likewise, it delivers us from the affliction of "vain repetition." Instead of saying the same thing over and over, we can follow God's word. When we engage in praying the scriptures, the word of God guides our praying, rather than our guiding the prayer time with our own thoughts and prayers. Often we try to come up with what to pray, but God has already provided for us what we need to pray through His holy word.

What else does praying the scriptures do for us? How can we benefit from this simple, but profound method of prayer? When we pray the scriptures, we have focus, guidance, confidence, strength, and help in time of need and prayer. One of the results we find in praying the scripture is it will help get us unstuck in our prayer time. When there are no other words to utter, we can always depend on God's word.

As we pray the scriptures, we learn to be intentional about what we are praying and have the opportunity to apply God's word to our lives, reinforced with prayer. There are several ways we can practice this method of prayer:

1. Pray exactly what the scripture has and pray it back to God with passion and faith. This can easily be done through the Psalms. Paul's Epistles and the General Epistles in the New Testament are also useful for praying the scriptures.

2. Incorporate scripture within a general prayer, pour out your heart to God, and allow God to transform your heart with His word through prayer.

3. Meditate on the word of God and let the scriptures speak to you, and ask God, "What are you saying to me through Your word?" This is intentional listening for God's voice through His Holy word.

4. Use the scriptures to make them relevant for the times that we are living in. This will help you to apply God's word and prayer to our daily lives.

The word of God, along with the Spirit of God, brings prayer alive! As we pray the scriptures, we better understand them. Through these various methods of praying the scriptures, they can provide for us a more balanced prayer life. As you engage in this method of prayer, it is my prayer that you will draw closer to God, claim His promises in His word, and live out what we pray with the help of the Lord. Throughout life, we will often try various methods of prayer and numerous styles, but we have not prayed effectively until we have learned to pray the scriptures.

Let us conclude that praying God's word brings us in line with God's will, keeps us from praying selfishly, helps us to stay on course when praying, and strengthens our faith because of the promises of God. In addition, praying the scriptures gives us a model and a guide for prayer and adequate words when no others are available. When we pray God's word, we can always expect results! We can live in holy expectation from praying God's word because God always backs up His word. Praying the scriptures is a constant reminder that God's word keeps us right in the center of God's will.

Prayer:

Thank you Lord for giving us your Holy Word! It is indeed "a lamp unto our feet, and a light unto our path." We are able to study your word and live out your word, but we are also thankful that we can pray Your word! Help us to keep Your word close and even to "hide it in our hearts that we might not sin against you" (Psalm 119:11). Teach us how to pray and live Your word in practical ways. I also pray that Your word will guide my life and my prayers daily. I ask that you will give me the wisdom and the understanding of Your word so that I do not misuse, abuse, or confuse Your word in my prayer time with you. This I ask in Jesus' name, Amen!

Prayer Activity (The Practice of Praying The Scriptures)

I. Praying God's Word (Three Practical Ways)

    A. *Meditate On The Word*-(Example Scripture: Matthew 26:41)

This method of praying the scriptures is reading the scripture over and over and prayerfully meditating on its words. After much thought and time given to the scripture, ask the Lord, "What are you saying to me through this scripture and how can I apply it to my daily living?" This is pondering the word of God in our hearts and our minds. It is meditating upon the divine word of God and praying for spiritual insight and guidance.

B. Recall The Word (Incorporating Within Regular Prayer)
Waiting: Isaiah 40:31

Lord, Your word reminds us in Isaiah 40:31 that those who "wait upon you will renew their strength. We will mount upon wings as eagles, run and not be weary, walk and not faint" (KJV). At present in my life, I am having a difficult time waiting. I ask that You would help me to wait on You and to realize the power in hoping and trusting in You! Help me not to be impatient with You or others, but to totally depend upon You during this season of my life. I pray for not only patience, but for wisdom, strength, and perseverance so that I might live life according to Your will. May I be like the eagle, allow the storms of life to let me soar and thereby grow to spiritual maturity. This I pray in Jesus' name, Amen!

Warfare: Luke 10:18-19

Lord, Your word teaches me that You have given me authority over all the power of the enemy in your name and nothing shall by any means hurt me. I want to first of all thank You for the spiritual authority through Your name that You have given me over the enemy. Second of all, I claim the authority in Jesus' name over demons, disease, disaster, depression, distractions, despair, and discouragement! I bind any strongholds in my life that the enemy Satan has put upon me and I have accepted. I now claim by faith deliverance, healing, hope, faith, power, joy, diligence, and encouragement through the blood and precious name of Jesus! Thank You, Lord, for protecting me and reminding me through Your word that I am more than a conqueror through the Lord Jesus Christ. This I pray in Jesus' name, Amen!

Witnessing: Acts 1:8

Dear Lord, Your word teaches us to be witnesses in Jerusalem, Judea, Samaria, and the uttermost parts of the earth. Lord, help me to take this calling and mandate seriously. Help me to daily be a true witness for You by being a faithful witness for You. Help me to share the good news of your life, ministry, death, burial, resurrection, and second coming with others. Lord, I ask that You will not only give me the passion to share my faith in You but also the power to share my faith in You! Lord, I pray that daily You will guide me to someone who needs to hear about You and what You did for all of us at Calvary. Dear Jesus, I pray that I will share the good news at home, at work, at church, and throughout the community where I live. May I never become so localized that I refuse to share the gospel with people outside of my own limited circle. Help me wherever I go to spread the wonders of Your saving power! Lord, I am at your call to respond to someone who does not know You. In Jesus' name, Amen.

C. Praying The Word (Reading Exactly What The Word Says or Making The Prayer Fit Your Situation.)

II. Praying The Word From The Psalms

For these areas of scriptures, you can spend time just reading and claiming God's word for your life and the situation that you might be facing at present. Whatever phase of life you might be in, God's word has provided a solution to every case. Allow the word of God to be a constant companion with the Holy Spirit to lead, rule, and guide your life daily as you pray.

- A. (Psalm 145:1-7) ADORATION (more in chapter six)
- B. (Psalm 51:1-12) CONFESSION (more in chapter seven)
- C. (Psalm 138: 1-4) THANKSGIVING (more in chapter twelve)
- D. (Psalm 70) SUPPLICATION (more in chapter eight)

III. Praying in the New Testament

- A. The Lord's Prayer-Luke 11: 1-4
    - 1. Adoration
    - 2. Submission
    - 3. Provisions

4. Confession

5. Forgiveness

6. Protection

B. Praying For Spiritual Blessings-Ephesians 3: (Pray out this scripture as Paul does)

C. Ephesians Chapter 4:1-3-Praying For the Body of Christ

1. Pray for godly character

2. Pray for humility

3. Pray for unity

4. Pray for peace

5. Pray for love

D. Praying through the fruit of the spirit for spiritual growth-Galatians 5: 22-23

1. Love

2. Joy

3. Peace

4. Longsuffering

5. Goodness

6. Gentleness

7. Faithfulness

8. Meekness

9. Self-Control

IV. There are numerous areas throughout the scriptures that we can use to pray, such as praying for guidance (2 Chronicles 20:3-9), praying to break strongholds (2 Corinthians 10:4-5), or using the Psalms as prayers for devotional and praying them back to God (Psalms 22, 23, 24, 27, 34, 37 and numerous others).

V. Take some time to write in a prayer journal (a spiral composition notebook or loose leaf paper in a three ring binder will suffice). In the journal, write a prayer using one of your favorite scriptures that may speak to your present situation, and pray it back to God. Quietly wait for God's response.

Study Questions:

1. Why is it so important to pray the scriptures?
2. In what way can the word of God help us in our prayer life?
3. Has praying the scriptures ever worked for you or helped you? Expound.
4. How are Psalm 119 and prayer related?
5. How can meditating on God's word strengthen your prayer life as well as your walk with the Lord?
6. Why is the will of God important in prayer?
7. How can praying the scriptures give us a more balanced prayer life?

CHAPTER FOUR

THE PRAYER LIFE OF JESUS: IF JESUS PRAYED, WHAT ABOUT US?

—⟨₰₰₰⟩—

While there are many wonderful people throughout history who have been noted as people of prayer, the greatest example of a life of prayer can be found in the life and person of the Lord Jesus Christ. Many of us are familiar with the prayers of Moses, David, Jabez, Daniel, Solomon, Samson, Hannah, Anna, and many others. We are also acquainted with the Lord's Prayer, but the prayer life of Jesus is so in tune to the will of God that it is hard to image such a lifestyle of prayer in one individual.

Jesus Christ while on earth was a person of prayer! Although we do not always know what He said, we do know that constantly

He prayed. There were numerous types of prayers uttered by Jesus. His prayers were relational because He prayed to be in communion with His Father and offered prayers that would glorify God. He prayed and interceded on behalf of others, He prayed privately, He prayed publicly, He prayed in the daytime, He prayed in the nighttime, and He prayed anytime! He prayed before He raised Lazarus from the dead (John 11:41-42); He prayed for Peter before he denied Him (Luke 22:31-32); and He prayed a High Priestly prayer for unity in the church (John 17).

Throughout the gospels, we find Jesus Christ in the regular habit of prayer. To prove this point further, Luke 5:16 notes, "But Jesus often withdrew himself to lonely places and prayed" (NIV). Prayer for Jesus was not occasional, but often. It was more than habit, but His life. Perhaps prayer was to Jesus what eating, sleeping, and taking a bath are to us. It is the necessity for life and ministry. Prayer to Jesus was more than just asking for things, but also spending time alone with His Father! When Jesus prayed, He prayed Kingdom prayers, prayers that would advance the Kingdom of God! His prayers were those that would transform, heal, deliver, encourage, and cause marvelous events in individual's lives that would also bring them closer to God!

As we view the scriptures, we discover that Jesus Christ was a busy man, but never too busy to pray! The more the crowds came, the more Jesus prayed. The more the fame came, the more Jesus prayed. The more the opposition came, the more Jesus prayed. The more intense things became, the more Jesus prayed. He stayed in close communication with His Father. Jesus would withdraw himself from human sight and contact. The modern day Christian has a great challenge, and that is to fall in love more with the approval of God than we do the praise and the compliments of people. Should we not prefer quiet and quality time with the Lord rather than the applause of others? The gospels record not only Jesus reaching the lost and meeting the needs of others, but also praying! If the Lord Jesus Christ prayed, what makes us think we can go through life without praying? Jesus was perfect and providential, but He prayed. As we study the prayer life of Jesus, we see that He prayed on purpose and He prayed *with* purpose. There was always a divine intent in His praying.

Let's consider now the prayer life of Jesus Christ. He often withdrew Himself to lonely places and prayed. As we encounter Jesus' prayer life at various phases of Jesus' life and ministry, we see Jesus withdrawing often to lonely places and praying. We view Jesus praying as He starts His earthly ministry and as He serves in ministry. We also find Jesus praying as He struggles and surrenders, but He does it all through His relationship with His Father. Jesus is intentional about praying and connecting with the Father. As Jesus spent time in prayer, He practiced solitude, stillness, and silence. Therefore, if Jesus prayed, what about us?

Jesus Practiced Solitude

We read that "He withdrew Himself . . . ." Jesus left the crowd. While the crowds for Jesus were great and there were many demands, He often withdrew Himself and practiced solitude. Jesus would get away from people not because He didn't love people, but so that He could continue to care for and love people. Jesus left the crowd, as popular as He was, and went to commune with His Father. If He practiced solitude, a time of breaking away from the people, then what about us? There is a great lesson here, especially for those who serve before the crowd. We live in a busy world. Everybody is in a hurry going somewhere or nowhere. We're worn out, exhausted, and hard to deal with because we are tired. This comes about because we try very hard to be everything to everybody and do everything all the time. We need solitude so that we can spend one on one time with God. Being in the presence of God is a lot more important than being in the presence of people. When we have rested in solitude, we can come away refreshed and able to see life and ministry with a fresh set of eyes. Solitude also allows us to offer ourselves and all of our struggles up to God. Jesus did it, and so must we.

Jesus Practiced Stillness

Jesus not only withdrew Himself, but He also "withdrew to lonely places" or the wilderness. While solitude is breaking away from people, stillness is breaking away from activities. Jesus found a place away from the hustle and bustle of life. It's almost as if Jesus would go on a private retreat. He broke away from his regular routine of life and ministry to take care of the most important matter in ministry, never being too busy to spend time with His Father. Jesus practiced stillness because I believe He was trying to teach us how it ought to be done. He teaches us the power of stillness. When was the last time we just sat in the presence of God in a lonely place without any interruptions or distractions? Jesus did it, and if He Jesus did it, what about us? Someone once noted that "the enemy to intimacy is busyness!" From my own experience, when we are overworked and overextended, our fuse is short, and we have very little patience with ourselves and others. It's a good indicator that it's time to get still.

While God is calling us to do ministry, He is also calling us to Him! He calls us to calm down, slow down, wind down, lay down, and to sit down, to rest up and renew for the journey. If the devil can't stop us from doing God's work, he will try to kill us in it. The enemy will cause us to get in the rat race without ever resting, renewing, recovering, reviving, or replenishing. There will always be something to do in ministry. We will never catch up in ministry; therefore, we must do what we can while we can and then rest. If we learn to practice stillness like Jesus and take a retreat to enjoy the sweet presence of God, whatever we left will be there when we get back. We will never solve all of the problems in the family, the church, the community, the city, the state, the country, or the world. We can make our contribution, but if God does not fix some of what we are facing in the world, nobody will. Therefore, let us engage in life as Jesus did. If Jesus practiced stillness and prayer, shouldn't we?

Jesus Practiced Silence

"Jesus withdrew Himself to a lonely place and prayed . . . ." (Luke 5:16). Jesus not only broke away in solitude and stillness, but also in silence. He broke away from the noise and the voices that were around Him. Mark 6:31 records Jesus saying to His disciples, "Come ye yourselves apart into a desert place, and rest a while . . ." (KJV). Jesus knew the power of quietness and rest along with solitude and stillness. All three of these are associated with the prayer life of Jesus. Jesus not only practiced solitude and stillness, but He practiced silence through prayer. He would often commune with the Father. This business of silence teaches us that prayer is more than yelling at Jesus; it is also getting quiet and discerning the still, small voice of God. (It's like sitting at His feet in chapter four). Jesus knew the power of staying in close and keeping constant connection with His Father. He never sought to run ahead of Him to do His own thing.

Jesus broke away to pray because He knew that His instructions came from His Father and not from Himself. Jesus knew how to get quiet. Meditative prayer, quiet prayer, praying in the presence of God is what is going on here. He is sitting quiet in God's presence! It's no secret; we live in a noisy world. Everybody has something to say. All of us have an opinion. There are times when we need a rest from noise so that we can get quiet to hear the Lord. Silence means more than closing our mouths, but also silencing our minds and our spirits to be open to the voice of the Holy Spirit. Sometimes the mind can be racing away even when we are quiet. The reason we must rest in silence is because the Lord has some things He needs to say to each of us. Everybody needs a quiet place, a throne room, to hear God's voice. When we have heard God's voice, we can easily discern strange and inauthentic voices. There are times we don't need to say anything; we just need to be quiet. In silence, we pray and we listen. When we get silent, then we can get still, and when we are silent and still, solitude flows in. If you want to know God's will for your life, need some directions or some answers, or you need to improve your prayer life, look at Jesus! May we learn to pray more like Jesus! If Jesus prayed, how about us? If Jesus practiced solitude, shouldn't we? If Jesus practiced stillness, then what about us? If Jesus practiced silence, then what about us? Let us be diligent in spending time with Him as He did with His Father through solitude, stillness, and silence.

Praying Like Jesus

This portion of the chapter helps us to clearly understand Jesus praying at different phases of His life and ministry. As we view four New Testament events that speak to the prayer life of Jesus, we can grasp a clearer vision of the prayer life of Jesus Christ. Jesus prays when He is starting ministry, serving in ministry, struggling in ministry, and when He is surrendering in ministry. Jesus is prayed up, and He prays through!

Jesus Prays As He Starts His Earthly Ministry

As we continue to look at the prayer life of Jesus, we see Jesus praying as He begins His earthly ministry. Luke 3:21-22 records, "When all the people were being baptized, Jesus was baptized too. And as He was praying, heaven opened. And the Holy Spirit descended on Him in bodily form like a dove" (NIV). Jesus begins ministry with prayer and the power of the Holy Spirit. As Jesus is preparing for His earthly ministry, He is being baptized by John the Baptist but commissioned by His Father. Jesus prays and the heavens open! We do not know what He prayed, but we know it was effective. He prayed, the Holy Spirit came in the form of a dove, God was well-pleased, and the Holy Spirit drove Him into the wilderness. He did not select a disciple until He had spent forty days in prayer and fasting. He prays as He begins an awesome earthly ministry! The prayer lesson for us is that no task in life or ministry should begin without prayer. Jesus exemplifies to us the importance of prayer and ministry. It appears that they both go hand in hand. If ministry is to be effective, it must be effected with prayer. Perhaps as we serve in ministry, prayer should be such a vital part of us until we do nothing without the blessings and authority of God. If Jesus Christ prayed in this manner, what about in our lives and ministry? Even as Jesus moves forward in ministry, He is purposeful and intentional about prayer. Should we not be intentional about praying as we set out to begin a ministry task as Jesus was? Several things happened when Jesus prayed in this passage: the heavens opened up, the Holy Spirit descended, and the voice of God was heard.

When Jesus Prayed the Heavens Opened Up

After Jesus prayed, the Heavens opened up. We think of heaven as up! It has been known as the dwelling place of God. But we also think of heaven as the sky. The sky was opened. When we think of the heavens opening up, we think of the blessings of God coming down. When the heavens open up, there is an anticipation that God is about to do something. When Jesus prayed, the heavens opened. Could it be said that when we pray earnestly and sincerely that the heavens will open up for us? There was a divine intervention in heaven on Jesus' behalf. There is no doubt that we live in a time when we need divine interventions on our behalf. We live in a day and time when we need for the heavens to open up. We need prayers like Jesus' that will cause heaven to open up. As we are faced with war, terrorism, the economy, the problems in the Middle East, health care, mortgage foreclosures, and many other issues in our country, state, city, community, and the church, we need for heaven to open up. Prayer can open up heaven as it did for Jesus!

When Jesus Prayed the Holy Spirit Came Down

We see that when the heaven open, the Holy Spirit of God was released to Jesus after prayer. When the heavens opened, the Holy Spirit came down. The Holy Spirit descended from heaven in the form of a dove. The Holy Spirit is God in spirit, who reigns in the earth to equip, empower, and encourage the people of God in ministry. The Holy Spirit is co-equal with God the Father and His only Son, Jesus Christ, yet distinct from them. It is important that the Holy Spirit descended upon Jesus in the form of a dove because it teaches us that not only must prayer be a central part of life and ministry, but so also should be the presence of the Holy Spirit. The Holy Spirit is the *ruach* in Hebrew, the wind or the breath of God. The Holy Spirit gives life, strength, and guidance to the people of God. The Holy Spirit bears fruit, builds ministry, brings hope and unity, restores joy, revives people renews churches, rebuilds communities, and replenishes life.

The Holy Spirit also has the ability to give gifts. Although there are many gifts, there is only one spirit. Let me hasten to say that while the Holy Spirit gives gifts for ministry, the Holy Spirit does more than offer us gifts for the ministry: the Holy Spirit empowers us to live right with the fruit of the Holy Spirit—love, joy, peace, meekness, longsuffering, faithfulness, goodness, gentleness, and self-control. If Jesus prayed and the Holy Spirit came down, we need to pray that the Holy Spirit will manifest among us and do a work in us, through us, with us, and for us, as done with Jesus, so that the Kingdom of God can come and the will of God can be done. What would happen to the Christian movement of today if we sincerely prayed until the heavens opened up? What revelation, what power, and what miracles we would experience!

When Jesus Prayed, the Voice of God Was Heard

After the heavens opened and the Holy Spirit came down, the people all heard the voice of God. There comes a time in prayer when we must listen for the voice of God. As the Holy Spirit speaks to us, we are guided by the Holy Spirit through prayer, fasting, the word of God, and the people of God who will often confirm God's voice already spoken to us. When God speaks, we must know that He has spoken, and we must know what He has said. The Lord spoke by saying, "This my beloved Son in whom I am well pleased" (Luke 3:22, KJV). The Father speaks out of a relationship. Relationship is what prayer is all about. Notice that Jesus does nothing to gain the approval of His Father except spending time with Him. What God wants out of us first and foremost—before ministry, before money, before anything else—

is a personal relationship with Him. He is never more pleased with us than when we are hanging out with Him! Intimacy!

We live in a day when we need to hear the voice of God. There are many strange voices and strange doctrines floating around, but if we pray as Jesus did, we will also begin to hear the voice of God through the Holy Spirit. May we pray until we hear clearly the peaceful, powerful, and protective voice of God! God spoke then, and He speaks now. If prayer can be that powerful for Jesus Christ, then how much more powerful can it be for us? If Jesus prayed, then what about us? May we learn to pray like Jesus!

Jesus Prays While Serving In Ministry

From this place we find Jesus praying while He is serving in ministry. This scripture teaches us that "Very early in the morning, while it was still dark, Jesus got up, left the house and went off to a solitary place and prayed." (Mark 1:35, NIV). At this point, Jesus has selected only a few of His disciples, but His ministry is flourishing already! He has a large following; nevertheless, in the midst of the crowd, he gets up very early in the morning to pray. Undoubtedly, while the crowds are still asleep, Jesus is praying. Ministry for Jesus is flourishing, but in the midst of flourishing ministry, He is praying! Jesus is healing, helping, teaching, preaching, leading, guiding, and directing, and in the midst of it all, He Prays! Jesus serves, but while He is serving and helping others, He does not neglect the discipline of prayer. Jesus prays in the midst of ministry, and Jesus prays as He continues His ministry.

When Jesus Prays, He Prays In the Midst of Ministry (verse 35)

(Notice: He gets up a great while before day.) He gets up perhaps while others are asleep. He fights the temptation of sleeping in and cutting His prayer time short. But before the crowds gather, He meets with His Father. Yes, ministry is moving forward and He really does not have time to pray, but He takes the time to pray. In ministry there is always something to do, someone to see, somewhere to go, a sermon to preach, a lesson to teach, a song to sing, a meeting to attend, a person to encourage, etc. But like Jesus in the midst of it all, we must take the time to pray. We are often encouraged to pray when things are not going well, but from following Jesus, we are likewise encouraged to pray when things are going well. Whether life and ministry are blooming or gloomy, prayer should be the order of the day as was with Jesus. When things are going well, it is easy to neglect the Lord and worship the gifts, the benefits, and blessings that the ministry brings. Instead,

Jesus stayed focused in prayer while serving in a thriving ministry.

From my own personal experience, ministry and service to the Lord can often distract our prayer time with Him. We see a tremendous example of a life balanced with prayer and ministry through Jesus Christ. Jesus teaches us how to not only work for the Lord, but to also let the Lord work with us, through us, in us, and for us! Praying while we are serving teaches us that, as we give out in ministry, we should also receive ministry and strength from the Lord to continue. As Jesus refreshed, renewed, and reconnected, so must we through the practice of prayer. I believe that one of the tactics of Satan is to keep us so busy that we can't pray. No matter how well things are going, we must never neglect the ministry and discipline of prayer because then we are too busy for God. The lesson is to pray even when ministry is thriving and Jesus did.

When Jesus Prays, He Prays and Continues His Mission

In reading Mark 1:36-39, Jesus continues His ministry after He pauses for prayer. He prays and continues His ministry. Notice that He prays and then He preaches. He prays in the middle of preaching, He preaches in between prayers. Likewise, He delivers those who are bound, and He heals those who are sick. He prays and He delivers! He prays and He heals! What a wonderful model Jesus gives us in ministry to develop the habit of not neglecting prayer, or the assignment! Prayer is not a substitute for work; it is connected with the work. Work is not a substitute for prayer; it is connected with prayer. After we pray, we must obey. We must pray and then do what the Lord directs us to do. Praying does not exempt us from doing what God called us to do; rather, it empowers us to do that which God has assigned for us to do. The more work we have to do, the more praying we must do; but we must never neglect one over the other. Jesus did His praying and He did His work. Jesus teaches us a ministry balance of prayer and work! He prays before work, He prays in between work, and He prays after work. Let us on this journey, learn to pray like Jesus. Thus, If Jesus prayed, what about us? If Jesus prayed while He was serving, then we must pray also.

Jesus Prays While Struggling In Ministry

This segment of the chapter shows Jesus praying while He is struggling with ministry. Ministry is not always easy! Yes, ministry can be rewarding at times, but at other times it can be a struggle. What does it mean to struggle? It is to contend with an adversary or to put forth a great deal of energy with an opposing force. It is to do something difficult. Thus was the case in this text with the

Lord Jesus Christ. Luke 22:41-42 records, "He withdrew about a stone's throw beyond them, knelt down and prayed, 'Father, if you are willing, take this cup from me; yet not my will, but yours be done'" (NIV). An angel from heaven appeared to Him to strengthen Him. "And being in anguish, he prayed more earnestly, and his sweat was like drops of blood falling to the ground" (NIV). Jesus is battling in the flesh with an eternal weight. Jesus struggles with facing crucifixion and death. This type of prayer appears to be one of the most difficult prayers Jesus has ever prayed. All prayers are not the easy type to pray. Some prayers are "I don't want to do this," "I don't want to let go, but I don't want to hold on either." There are some prayers we pray, and we ask the Lord to relieve us from a difficult assignment, job, or relationship. This is where Jesus is in the Garden of Gethsemane. It's a tough place to be. I contend that He is between "a rock and a hard place." He has to do what He doesn't want to do, and He has to face the inevitable. He is struggling between pleasing His Father and pleasing Himself. Jesus battles with saving sinful humanity and saving His spotless self. Nevertheless, He prays, "If it be thy will, let this cup pass from me." Jesus is holding on in the natural to what God has been doing in the spiritual. The struggle is great! The struggle is so great until, His sweat becomes a bloody sweat.

Praying and letting go in life is not always easy. The struggles of life can often weigh us down, and we have to learn to pray, even when we are struggling. Praying and struggling go hand in hand. It's impossible to fully understand the struggle without persevering in prayer.

Numerous Christians believe that the greatest battle for Jesus was not at Calvary, but in the Garden of Gethsemane. By the time He got to Calvary, His mind was already made up. Jesus prayed through the struggle because His struggle was for a greater cause than Himself. For a moment, Jesus appears to be stuck in a rut but willingly submits to His Father's will. If prayer helped Jesus when He was stuck, it will also help us when we are struggling, straining, and stressing with the cares and disappointments of life. Praying in the struggle and through the struggle teaches us to hold on to God and prayer, especially in the difficult decisions and seasons of life. Thus, if Jesus prayed in times of struggle, what about us?

Jesus Prays while Surrendering in Ministry

This prayer is the last of the seven words of Jesus from the Cross. "Jesus called out with a loud voice, 'Father, into your hands I commit my spirit'" (23:46, NIV). Watching Jesus praying and struggling at Gethsemane reveals victory at the cross as He totally surrenders to the will of God! "When he had said this, he breathed His last" (Luke 23:46, NIV). Jesus has moved from a place of struggle, to a place of surrender! It all takes place through the practice of prayer. The Lord has done His work, fulfilled His earthly mission and now He gives Himself back to His Father. Even at death, Jesus is praying. What a blessed way to die, with a prayer in your heart and on your lips! He has pleased His Father! Jesus has been beaten, slapped, mocked, spit upon, wounded, bruised, pierced, ridiculed, abandoned, and crucified. He had already cried, "It Is Finished" (John 19:30, KJV). Now He cries, "Father into thy hands I commit my spirit . . . ." Notice that Jesus does not pray, "Father, I quit!" But He prays to surrender! Surrendering does not mean giving up, but submitting to a greater authority. Jesus totally surrenders! Surrender alone is not the most important thing, but the most important thing is to whom He surrendered! Let's look at Jesus praying in His dying hour: "Father into thy hands I commit my spirit and having said thus, He gave up the ghost." (Luke 23:46, KJV). Jesus prays a prayer of commitment, and then He prays a prayer of contentment.

When Jesus Prays To Surrender, He Prays A Prayer of Commitment (Father, into your hands I commit my spirit)

He utters Psalm 31:5, "Into thine hand I commit my spirit: thou hast redeemed me, O Lord God of truth" (KJV). This was the prayer that every Jewish mother taught her child to pray before going to sleep at night. It's like the prayer many of us were taught growing up: "Now I lay me down to sleep, I pray the Lord my soul to keep; if I should die before I wake, I pray the Lord my soul to take." It is almost as if Jesus is falling asleep in His father's arms, without a worry, care, or concern. He has done His work and now places Himself into the total hands of Almighty God. He has redeemed humanity, and He is safe. Jesus commits Himself to the loving care of His Father. He has already committed Himself in life and ministry, and now He commits Himself in death. There comes a time in life and ministry that some things we just have to turn over to the Lord. Sometimes we struggle long, we struggle hard, we hold on, and we hold on tight. At times, we keep a tight hold on things; on ourselves, and sometimes others, and there comes a day when the Lord says, you've held on to this long enough, it's time let go and let me handle this matter. This kind of praying is when we commit every situation we have to the Lord and trust that He is going to work it out. Jesus teaches us the power of prayer in surrender.

When Jesus Prays To Surrender, He Prays a Prayer of Contentment (having said thus, He gave up the ghost)

The death of Jesus Christ at Calvary moves us to a place of humility and gratitude. He has completed His assignment and has pleased His Father. For Jesus, the suffering is over, and He has given a cry of victory! He did not come down, Elijah did not save Him, Angels did not rescue Him, and abuse did not stop Him. Judas did not intimidate Him, suffering did not detour Him, and the mob did not frighten Him. Thorns, spears, nails, and a whip did not hinder Him. He endured the pain, the suffering, and the agony without murmuring, whining, or complaining. Jesus Christ is in a place of contentment because His mission is accomplished. It is fitting that Jesus utters the words, "It is finished" just before, "Father into thy hands I commend my spirit" because there is always a restlessness and an uneasiness in one's heart until one has accomplished their divine assignment. Jesus dies with the prayer on His lips.

There is power in surrender. Nevertheless, He surrenders to a life of Resurrection and Power three days later! As Jesus surrenders, He teaches us that new life, power, and resurrection come when we totally surrender to the will of Almighty God! We discover from this kind of prayer that we must learn to pray prayers of surrender from one season in life and ministry to another. There are different seasons in ministry. We see this from watching the life of Jesus.

There comes a time when we must be sensitive to the change in ministry. Praying to surrender to God's will and a change of season will assist us in not fighting to keep things the way they are when God is trying to change us and our season.

In conclusion, Jesus teaches us what it really means to "pray without ceasing." No matter what the case, He is praying! He prays while He is starting ministry, He prays while He is serving in ministry, He prays while He is struggling in ministry, and He prays while He is surrendering in ministry. Jesus is praying at every turn of life. He becomes the prayer example for every believer! No matter where we find Jesus in the Gospels, who He is with, or what He is doing, the discipline of prayer is close at hand. We learn from Jesus Christ that whatever we are going through, we must learn to pray through. Praying through will help each Christian mature in every situation and circumstance in life as we desire to be more like Jesus. The real prayer model and prayer warrior is Jesus Christ! If we want to know how it ought to be done, watch Jesus, follow Jesus, listen to Jesus, and obey Jesus. Whatever we need to know about life and prayer, Jesus has already modeled for us. O for a people who would be willing to pray like Jesus! What the Lord teaches us is that, there is never a season in our lives when we should cease praying. Even when we are in a season of rest, renewal, and refreshing, we should be in a mode of prayer. As we carry out every assignment, our hearts, minds, and attitudes should be God-focused. Jesus has taught us the purpose and power of prayer. He has been the model that shows us how to get and stay connected with God; His purpose and His ways, and experience the manifestation of His power through prayer. For that reason, "If Jesus prayed, what about us?"

Prayer Response:

Dear Lord Jesus, I am amazed at how intentional you were with your prayer life while on earth. No matter how busy, challenged, or opposed you were, you devoted yourself to a lifestyle of prayer. You have provided us with an example that we should always find time to pray. I pray Luke 11:1 as your disciples prayed: "Teach me to pray as John also taught his disciples." I desire to be more like you in my prayer life. I pray for the wisdom, strength, and perseverance to pray like you! This I ask in Your Wonderful Name, Amen!

Study Questions:

1. Why do you believe it is important to understand the prayer life of Jesus Christ?

2. What do you sense would cause Jesus to get up before day to pray? Explain.

3. Do you believe it is important to live a lifestyle of prayer like Jesus? Why or Why not?

4. What four different ways do you find Jesus praying in this chapter? How do they affect your life?

5. How intentional was Jesus Christ in His prayer life?

Practical Prayer Application:

In your journal, write your own prayer response to following Jesus' lifestyle of prayer. Be sure to include what you sense the Holy Spirit is saying to you.

CHAPTER FIVE

PRAYING DISCIPLES

Prayer is a means of communicating with and spending time with God. For many people, the only method of prayer is asking, seeking, knocking, and finding. While, Matthew 7:7-8 does imply asking and Philippians 4:6 commands us to make our petitions and request known to God, prayer is more than making requests. Prayer is being aware of God's power, purpose, presence, protection, provisions, and peace. Prayer keeps us in touch with the character and attributes of God! Howard Thurman writes, "Prayer is a form of communication between God and man *(humanity)* and man *(humanity)* and God. It is the essence of communication between persons that they shall talk with each other from the same basic agenda. Wherever this is not done, communication tends to break down."[3] From this we recognize that prayer keeps us connected with God. Family members, church members, and friends will often say to one another in their parting, "Stay in touch." This is the very essence of the prayer life of a Christian disciple. Prayer is "staying in touch." However, it is staying in touch with the best friend one could ever have. It is my assumption that the more we stay in touch with God, the more like Christ we become.

Because prayer is a wonderful Christian growth tool, if we become praying disciples, we can grow through the practice of prayer. While it is important for Christians to pray together, it is as equally important for one to pray alone. Spending private time with God can assist each Christian in growing in his or her walk with Christ.

In Luke 10: 38-42 is an account of two sisters named Martha and Mary. The city of this biblical scene is Bethany. Bethany is about two miles from Jerusalem. It lies on the eastern slope of the Mount of Olives. The Lord Jesus often preferred to stay in Bethany with Mary and Martha rather than in Jerusalem. They

---

[3] Howard Thurman, *Disciplines of the Spirit* (Friends United Press: Richmond, IN, 1963), 88.

had a brother named Lazarus, whom Jesus raised from the dead (John 11:38-44). Because of Jesus' love for this family, He often visited their home and enjoyed their warm hospitality.

"As Jesus and his disciples were on their way, he came to a village where a woman named Martha opened her home to him. She had a sister called Mary, who sat at the Lord's feet listening to what He said. But Martha was distracted by all the preparations that had to be made. She came to him and asked, 'Lord, don't you care that my sister has left me to do the work by myself? Tell her to help me!' 'Martha, Martha, you are worried and upset about many things, but one thing is needed. Mary has chosen what is better and it will not be taken away from her.'" Luke 10:38-42 (NIV)

Martha seems to be the older, hardworking type, who is always busy. Mary resembles the serene type who will work, but not while Jesus is present. "Mary sat at Jesus' feet and heard His words" (Luke 10:39). Mary and Martha both are lovers of Jesus, but Martha appears to be more concerned about service than time with Jesus. Martha becomes upset and seeks Mary's help.

Martha is disturbed because it seems that Jesus does not care about what she is undergoing. Her question was "Lord don't you care that my sister has left me to serve alone? Make her come and help me" (Luke 10:40). Martha is deeply troubled about getting things ready. She is anxiously working while Mary is sitting. The task is great for Martha so she seeks to rebuke Mary by talking to Jesus about her. Jesus responds with wisdom and admonition. While Martha has allowed her own personality to take her in another direction, Mary is commended for choosing the good part, which is sitting at Jesus' feet. Active service is important but never at the expense of spending time with Jesus. Martha's struggle was that she did not know when to sit and became overwhelmed by her serving.

Martha represents Christians who are busy for the Lord but do not slow down to spend time with Him. Mary represents the vision the Lord has for His people. That desire is that every Christian would chose the "good part," which is spending time with Him. Service and food are fine in their place, but what feeds the soul is more important than what feeds the body. For the Christian today, it is easy to become involved in work without true worship.

It appears that Jesus is interfering with Martha's help in the kitchen. Outward service is temporal, but sitting at the feet of Jesus is eternal. Mary teaches us the power of prayer and worship. Martha teaches us the power of service. While service is much needed, prayer and fellowship with God are the greater need. Learning to choose the good part helps us to become spiritually intentional disciples. Mary sits, because she is aware of the blessing of being in the Lord's presence. Being in the Lord's presence is what makes work more meaningful!

In order to be intentional about prayer, prayer can be expressed in numerous ways. From viewing this biblical scene with Jesus, Martha, and Mary, we are led to look at prayer from three angles. We shall look at prayer as worship, prayer as discipleship, and prayer as fellowship. Each of these areas can be used to build or strengthen one's prayer life and cause growth in the life of a Christian disciple.

Prayer as Worship

Prayer is an act of worship. Prayer is an important part of the worship experience and not just an event. Prayer is a key component in worship both publicly and privately. Second Chronicles 7:14, implies that when one is humble, seeking, repentant, and God focused one can realize transformation in worship through prayer. When using prayer as a tool in worship there are the prayers of adoration, confession, thanksgiving, supplication, and intercession. Adoration sets the atmosphere for worship in prayer. It describes the attributes of God, His character, and His awesome power. In confession we recall our faults and repent of the sins that we have committed. Thanksgiving is a time to give thanks to God for recent and past blessings and deliverance. In supplication we petition God and request help in a difficult situation. It could also include intercession praying for the needs of other people.[4] Prayer as worship is speaking to God. It can be done through talking, singing, or praying the Holy Scriptures. The scriptures encourage "Let us then approach the throne of grace with confidence, so that we may receive mercy and find grace to help us in our time of need" (Hebrews 4:16, NIV). We are confident that if we pray and have faith in God, He hears us and is able to come to our rescue. As we seek to become more like Jesus Christ, praying as an act of worship can contribute greatly to our Christian maturity.

Prayer as Discipleship

Prayer used as discipleship is listening and meditating upon the word and voice of God. It is listening for the voice of God, and

---

[4] Bill Hybels, *Too Busy Not to Pray* (Intervarsity Press: Downers Grove, IL, 1998), 61–69.

seeking His direction. This aspect of prayer teaches us that prayer is a dialogue and not a monologue. However, discipleship prayer goes beyond dialog to change in the disciple. For many years, I heard the statement that "prayer changes things." However, while that is true, prayer also changes people, circumstances, as well as situations. Richard J. Foster writes in his book, *Prayer: Finding the Heart's True Home,*

> "Prayer changes things," people say. It also changes us. The latter goal is the more imperative. The primary purpose of prayer is to bring us into such a life of communion with the Father that, by the power of the Spirit, we are increasingly conformed to the image of the Son. This process of transformation is the sole focus of Formation Prayer. None of us will keep up a life of prayer unless we are prepared to change."[5]

If people are prepared to pray, they must also be prepared to change. Prayer has often brought about transformation in the lives of many people. Thomas Keating in *Open Heart, Open Mind,* notes that, "Prayer is not designed to change God, but to change

---

[5] Richard J. Foster, *Prayer: Finding The Heart's True Home,* (Harper San Francisco: New York, 1992), 57.

us."[6] Therefore, praying and change go together. When we sit to hear, it contributes to spiritual maturity. Howard Thurman calls this the prayer of silence.

Jesus Christ teaches us what is most important in the life of a Christian as He responds to Martha. The scripture puts it this way: "'Martha, Martha,' the Lord answered, 'you are worried and upset about many things, but only one thing is needed.' (verses 41–42). 'Mary has chosen what is better, and it will not be taken away from her.'" In this passage, we see that Martha loved to serve, but in her anxious manner of waiting on Jesus, she caused unrest. Mary, in her own simple style, waited on Jesus by sitting at His feet. She instinctively knew what the Master wanted most, which was her undivided attention. There are times when the Lord needs our undivided attention in the prayer closet. This is meditating upon the word of God, ceasing all striving and listening intently to the voice of the Lord. We can find great spiritual strength in this area of prayer through stillness (resting from activity), silence (resting from noise), and solitude (resting from people). Finding time to grow through prayer makes us better disciples for Jesus Christ.

---

[6] Thomas Keating, *Open Heart, Open Mind* (Continuum: New York, 2003), 62.

Prayer as Fellowship

When we think of fellowship, it is usually with other Christians. However, prayer can be designed as a means of fellowshipping with God. Prayer as fellowship is living in the presence of God. Otis Ledbetter calls it "The Secret Place (Psalm 91). It is recognizing that God is always around. Psalm 139:7-10, teaches that wherever one goes, God is there! There is no place one can go to escape the Almighty. Because God is everywhere, people are able to commune with Him anywhere and anytime. No one can get away from God. This implies that one does not need an appointment with God to pray.

Fellowship with God is a possibility for prayer. Time, place, or space does not limit fellowship with God. It is being in constant communion with God. This method of praying is cultivating our relationship with God through spiritual intimacy. Some scriptures where we learn about this are:

- "Enoch walked with God," Genesis 5:24
- "Moses encountered God," Exodus 3; 33:12-21
- "David remembered the power of God's presence" Psalm 16:11
- "Daniel prayed three times a day," Daniel 6:10

Those who serve and follow the Lord and stay connected with Him are aware of His constant presence. Through prayer, a more meaningful relationship is developed with God. Through worship, people talk to God; through discipleship, God speaks to His people; and in fellowship, Christians walk with God and enjoy His presence. Prayer is being in close communion with God because He is always around!

Mary helps us to understand that even before work there must be worship, discipleship, and fellowship through prayer. The effective growth of a Christian comes through spending time with the Lord. Therefore, we must learn to hear, sit, and choose as Mary did. What takes place in Luke 10:38-42 becomes reality for many of us. What happened with Mary and Martha often happens in the church, in families, and in the life of a Christian believer. Without attention to practical spirituality, we can become spiritually unbalanced and lose our focus. In my experience, out of balance disciples can become overburdened, overloaded, overwhelmed, and overactive. Without a strong and consistent prayer life we can easily become furious, fussy, and frustrated. The danger for disciples is becoming so busy with working for Jesus that they forget about walking and talking with Him.

In conclusion, the Lord calls us to serve Him and work for Him, but the first ministry is to sit at His feet, hear His words, and choose the good part, which shall not be taken away. I believe that the good part is prayer, and what we must learn about prayer is that it is good for anything. Prayer is the remedy for every malfunction in life, family, and ministry. All we do must be handled with prayer. As we sit, hear, and choose what God has for us, this makes us intentional praying disciples. Becoming praying disciples helps us to live and pray like Jesus. Just as farmers plant seeds and anticipate a harvest, prayer is planting seeds, and in God's own time, will, and way, we begin to see a harvest of our prayers. No matter what the outcome or the answer may be, we can expect God to respond to the lives and prayers of His disciples.

Prayer:

Dear Lord, help me to become a praying disciple. Please help me to be intentional daily about my relationship with you. Allow me to grow spiritually through prayer and intimacy. May I never get so busy working for you that I neglect to talk to you and to listen to you. Please teach me how to balance life and ministry so that I do not become overwhelmed with serving. I ask that you would guide me in sitting, listening, and choosing what pleases you. With your guidance I want to be able to choose the good part, which can never be taken away. My life needs more of you and less of me. I entrust my daily schedule to you so that I might be able to become the prayer warrior you intended for me to be. This I pray with thanksgiving, Amen!

Study Questions

1. At present, who am I more like, Mary or Martha? Explain.

2. Why did Martha seem overwhelmed by all the work needed to be done?

3. What pleased Jesus the most?

4. Why do you think Mary choose the good part? What was the good part?

5. How does Luke 10:38-40 relate to prayer?

Prayer Activity

1. Spend some time quietly reading a scripture and then pray through the scripture, asking the Lord to speak to you through His word. Write what you sense the Lord is saying from the scripture.

2. Another activity could be: Take some time and pray through each of the following: adoration, confession, thanksgiving, petition, intercession,

and meditation. Write down anything unusual and wonderful that happens during your time of prayer. Do you sense things changing or remaining the same? Explain in your own words.

CHAPTER SIX

BUT, WHEN YOU PRAY

s we view this passage of scripture, we discover that it is an imperative to pray and not merely a suggestion. Jesus gives a directive: not if we pray, but *when* we pray. As the practice of prayer was evident, intentional, and regular in the life of Jesus, it should also be evident in the life of the Christian believer. It is quite clear to me that private prayer is just as important as public prayer. Both are necessary, and one should not be done to the exclusion of the other. Nevertheless, private prayer appears to be the foundation for our public prayer life.

In Matthew 6, Jesus warns against doing things for the sake of doing them or doing them in vain. This text reminds us of doing things for a show or a compliment. Written in Matthew 6:5, "And when thou prayest, thou shalt not be as the hypocrites are: for they love to pray standing in the synagogues and in the corners of the streets, that they may be seen of men. Verily I say unto you, They have their reward" (KJV). While Jesus does not downplay public praying, He does warn about praying in a crowd to be seen, heard, or honored. What Jesus appears to communicate is if the only time He can hear from you is when you are in a crowd, there is no need to pray. If you are praying publicly for a compliment or a pat on the back, the praying is in vain. Private praying can be used to build up one's personal relationship and walk with the Lord. John Wesley realized that of all the spiritual disciplines, prayer is the chief of them all. Prayer keeps us close to the Father and enhances our walk with Him. Practicing the discipline of prayer teaches us that we are no longer dependent upon *ourselves* for growth, help, strength, and guidance, but upon the Lord.

When you pray, there are several things that come to mind from these verses of scripture. When you pray, find a closet, shut the door, and God will move. These verses suggest a progression in prayer. Prayer seems to be moving or going somewhere. Prayer is ultimately designed to talk with the Lord, but also for the Lord to talk with us. It is therefore a dialogue, rather than a monologue. Let's see how God works in our lives when we pray.

When You Pray, Find a Closet

"But thou, when thou prayest, enter into thy closet . . . ." (Matthew 6:6, KJV). This implies a closet as a place of seclusion, a secret place where and when you are alone with God. Your closet can be on a hill or in a hollow, on the mountain or in the valley. Your closet could be preparing a meal, the backyard, the living room, or some other special place. Your closet could be driving down the highway with no one in the vehicle but you and the Lord. Your closet could be in the bedroom or the bathroom. Likewise, your closet could be on a rock, a bench in a park, or on the lake, wherever you and God are alone. It could be on your feet or on your knees, sitting down or laying down—it does not matter the position of your body, as much as the position of the heart. We are moved to find a place, where you can hang out with God and commune with Him.

Personally, my greatest prayer closet time is walking on a track, in a mall, on a nature trail, or somewhere secluded, talking to God and listening for His voice. Everyone needs closet time with God. These are practical, intentional, and quality ways to spend time with God. There are days finding a closet and getting with God will mean more than just praying, but it becomes the most important appointment of the day.

When You Pray, Shut The Door

"And when you have shut the door, pray to thy father in secret
...." (Matthew 6:6, KJV). Here is where the separation of God and
people occur. There are some things you cannot tell anybody but
God. There some things that are better shared only with God. As
much of an asset and blessing that people can be, there are some
things about our lives other people will never understand. This
means that on some occasions, we must steal away like Jesus
did—away from family, friends, and associates—and tell God
what's on our hearts and our minds. There are times when you
have to turn off the cell phone, the television, and the computer, or
maybe even leave home, to get quiet with God. Shutting your door
means closing the world out and letting God in. It is giving God
our undivided attention with whatever matter we bring before
Him. Not only does God have our undivided attention, but we have
His as well! While we often have friends that we share personal
things with, there are things we share with God in private that are
not even shared with closest friends. Our family, friends, ministry
partners, and coworkers are wonderful to talk with. However,
there does come a time when the only conversation that will
suffice is the one with the Lord. We are reminded by the hymn
"What a Friend we Have in Jesus," which says, "What a friend we

have in Jesus, all our sins and griefs to bear, what a privilege it is to carry, everything to God in prayer." When we shut the door to the world, we can totally open our hearts to God. Nothing can be questioned by anyone when we shut the door with God. The closet of prayer is a place where only God can hear our heart, soul, and mind. It's a good place to take all of our cares and concerns.

When You Pray, God Will Move

". . . and thy Father which seeth in secret shall reward thee openly." (Matthew 6:6, KJV) This verse reveals to us that when we pray earnestly and openly, God answers prayer in a real and personal way! You don't have to tell anybody that you talked with the Lord, but the Lord will make it known to the entire world that you have been in His presence. He will reward you openly. (You get with God alone, but when God answers, those around you witness the evidence of prayer in your life). It's a private prayer that is accompanied by a public blessing! God does answer prayer! It may not always be the answer we want, but it will certainly be the answer we need: yes, wait, no, change, forgive, or perhaps it will be some other kind of directive the Lord will lead us in during this closet time of prayer. We must never underestimate the power of prayer or the level of response God will give to our prayers. He is certainly capable of taking private prayers and rewarding openly.

I remember very well a conversation we had in seminary one day on prayer. The instructor remarked that "if we are filled with the Holy Spirit and we pray by ourselves, then we are talking to ourselves." Because of my upbringing about prayer, this troubled me greatly. I left Salisbury, NC, and while driving back to Knoxville, TN, I pondered the statement during the entire four-hour drive. I thought about it during the weekend, even in my prayer time. I wondered if I was really talking to myself. Going back to seminary the next week, still considering the idea, I finally got resolve from the statement as we seminary students discussed this notion of "if we are filled with the Holy Spirit and if we pray by ourselves, then we are talking to ourselves." I came to this conclusion based on my own experiences with private praying: with as many times as I have prayed by myself and seen the results of prayers prayed being answered, then somebody somewhere must have been eavesdropping or spying on my prayer. With as many prayers as I have witnessed God answering, God got the word somehow that His child was in need, and He came to my rescue. There was someone around who made sure the Lord got the word that I was in need of His assistance. Somebody had to be eavesdropping because God is still answering prayers and moving in our lives. Therefore, when you pray, don't be afraid to ask God, don't be afraid to trust God, and be bold enough to believe that the God who sees in secret will reward you openly.

When you pray, don't forget His words; when you pray, don't forget His promises; when you pray, don't forget that God can and God will. Not only is God able, but He is willing. The following scriptures will affirm the validity and power of prayer:

- Jeremiah 33:3: "Call to me, and I will answer you, and show you great and mighty things, which you do not know" (NKJV).
- Isaiah 65:24: "And it shall come to pass, they before they call, I will answer, and while they are yet speaking, I will hear" (KJV).
- Luke 18:1: "We ought to always pray and not to faint" (KJV).
- Ephesians 6:18 "Praying always with all prayer and supplication with Spirit . . ." (KJV).
- Philippians 4:6: "Before careful for nothing, but in every thing by prayer and supplication, with thanksgiving, let your request be made known unto God" (KJV).
- I Thessalonians 5:17, "Pray without ceasing" (KJV).
- 1 Timothy 2:8: "I would that men pray everywhere, lifting up holy hands, without wrath and doubting" (KJV).

It is a known fact that when we pray, God still answers prayer! He comes to the aid of His children! He is always in time and on time! There will be many days when you call the Lord, and in His own way He will respond to your plea. So when you pray—not *if* you pray—find a closet, shut the door, and God will move. When you pray, pray until things change, pray until God works, pray until burdens are lifted, and pray until situations change! When you pray, pray until circumstances are transformed, and pray until you witness a mighty movement of God in your life! When you pray, pray until the forces of evil and darkness around you succumb to goodness and light; pray until God moves on your behalf; pray until peace, love, and joy have taken residence in your heart and the glory of God is shining through your life. When all else fails, pray and trust God to move. When you've done all of that, pray some more; persist and persevere in prayer until you see things changing about you. He's that kind of a God! May you become a person of prayer!

Prayer

Dear Lord, help me to understand the importance of spending time with you privately. May I never get so busy that I forget that the greatest relationship I have in this world is with you. Help me to practice prayer in my daily life and involve you in all that

I do. Guide me daily in the closet so that as I shut the world out momentarily, I can spend time with you in the secret place. Let me watch you at work and follow your commands in my life. Help me to bring all of my burdens that I cannot handle to You. I pray in Jesus' name, Amen.

Application and Activity

Get a prayer journal, write down your prayer requests, and go back later and see how God has answered them. Spend time studying Paul's exhortation on prayer in Ephesians 6:18, and use it as a model for your personal time of prayer.

I.   Pray Always

II.   Pray Different Ways

      a. Adoration, Praise, and Thanksgiving

      b. Confession and Repentance

      c. Supplication and Petitions

      d. Intercession

      e. Meditation and Quietness

III.   Pray In the Spirit

IV.   Pray With Watchfulness

V.   Pray With Perseverance

VI.   Pray For Others

Study Questions

1. What are some things in your life that you only feel comfortable talking to God about?

2. Is there anything in your life at present that you struggle to talk over with God?

3. Are there any areas not surrendered to God in your life? If so, pray about what the Lord would have you to do in response to them.

4. Why is closet prayer so important?

5. Can you think of a time you prayed in private and God came through for you? If so, recall it and give thanks to God.

CHAPTER SEVEN

ADORATION: GIVE GOD GLORY!

———∞∞∞———

This kind of prayer is what I call praying without complaints. It is strictly and intentionally ascribing glory and honor to God! The Prayer of Adoration is praying to God on His behalf and not for one's own benefit. It adores, admires, amplifies, acclaims and appreciates God. The Prayer of Adoration:

- Does not ask for anything.

- Does not pray for anybody.

- Does not seek for any answers.

- Does Honor God.

- Does Bless God.

- Does Exalt God.

This method of praying should be the first act of worship, whether in public or private. This prayer is never complete because there are not enough adjectives to describe how great and awesome one knows God to be. Psalm 145:1-4 (NIV) is a prayer of adoration because it lifts up God. It is a prayer that makes God look good! This is a prayer that adds weight to God! David exclaims this prayer of praise and adoration. Our prayer of adoration should always be Deliberate, Daily, and Delightful!

Deliberate Adoration

"I will exalt you, my God the King;

I will praise your name forever and ever." (145:1, NIV).

Here is a voluntary praise without error or fault not because another is praising God, but out of a close and personal relationship with Him. It is done without having been forced to adore God. He holds God in high regards; he raises and exalts God. We should adore God out of our willingness to pay tribute to a loving, kind, and faithful God. This lifts God up because of who He is and not what He does! This encourages us in our prayer time to do more than make requests. It moves us to offering to God through prayer intentional, continuous, and purposeful praise.

Daily Adoration

"Every day I will praise you and extol your

name forever and ever." (145:2, NIV).

It takes discipline to pray daily to make God look good. Each day one sees another side of God. Jeremiah declares that "His mercies are new every morning . . ." (Lamentations 3:23, KJV). New mercies call for new praise and adoration daily. Daily we have an opportunity to worship the God we love. The Psalmist is moved to adore God as a daily routine. He becomes a "habitual worshipper" to God. Daily we are to lift up the name and character of God. Whatever the day brings, we should praise God! God is wonderful even when life is not! Learning to worship and praise God in good times or sad times brings forth growth in those who follow the Lord. This teaches us that God deserves glory and adoration from us every day. Daily blessings provide daily opportunities to adore and praise God!

Delightful Adoration

"Great is the LORD and most worthy of praise;

his greatness no one can fathom. One generation will

commend your works to another; they will tell of

your mighty acts." Psalm 145:3-4, NIV)

The writer recognizes the greatness of God and resounds with such delight, "Great is the Lord and greatly to be praised." He is praying and worshipping with excitement, enthusiasm, zest and zeal. When we pray to make God look good, we find joy in praise and adoration. The delight is that no one knows all there is to know about God. Therefore, once we learn another attribute about God, we joyfully proclaim that God is great and greatly to be praised! One generation after another will delight in the power, majesty, presence and glory of God. We shall all rejoice and exclaim, "Bless the Lord, O my soul: and all that is within me, bless His holy name" Psalm 103 (KJV). One generation to the next should hear of the delightful ways we praise God. Communicating our praise not only to God but as a testimony for generations yet unborn glories God as well. May we in a delightful way discover exciting and creative ways to praise God!

The prayer of adoration should always describe to God His attributes. When we describe to God Who He is and what He means to us, worship comes alive! The following illustration describes worship and adjectives that may be used when praying this prayer to adore God.

I recall some time ago, I prepared dinner for the family. In my mind, it was a regular meal and nothing fancy. I do not remember the menu; however, my wife was deeply appreciative and continued complimenting me on a marvelous meal. Personally, I was not impressed with the meal, but she went back for more food. She repeatedly said, "This food is so good!" As she continued lifting up how good the food was, my mind immediately began to wonder, "What can I cook tomorrow to get this same kind of response?" She was so grateful that I felt that I owed her another meal, just for the warm compliment. I suppose that's what happens with God when we pray the prayer of adoration. When we proclaim to God that He is holy, that there is none like Him, and that He's the joy of our lives, God rejoices and delights in the praises of His people. When we pray to make God look good, we say, "Lord, you're my life, my joy, my hope, my peace, my way," and God begins to act and respond to our praise and worship. Our blessing God and adoring Him in turn blesses us with His presence and joy! Thus the challenge of today is to pray to make God look good. Go ahead and make your day by making God's day in praise and adoration. "O Magnify the Lord with me, and let us exalt His name together" (Psalm 34).

Prayer of Adoration

Dear Lord, how great, how loving, how kind, and how awesome You are! O Lord, how I adore and admire you! You are a fine friend, faithful Father, close companion, proficient provider, persistent protector, soul savior, and daily deliverer! You are one of a kind, and there is none like you any time or anywhere. I submit myself to you because you are trustworthy and worthy to be praised. You are Holy! You are Righteous! You are the best friend I've ever had! I am delighted to be one of your children. I love you, I need you, and I praise you and glorify your name! You are very dear and precious to me. You are the source of my strength, and you are my shield, my glory, and the lifter up of my head. In your mighty and awesome name of I pray. Amen.

Study Questions

1. Why type of prayer is found in this chapter? Expound on its significance.

2. How often should we give God praise, honor, and glory?

3. Why is it important that we praise God?

4. In what ways have you learned to praise and adore God?

Prayer Activity

✝ Spend time describing who God is. If possible, find a praise song: play, sing, or read it to God.

✝ Find a Psalm that adores and lifts up God and spend some quiet time worshipping God in song and with the Psalms.

✝ Spend a day praising God without any murmuring or complaining. Write down how a day without complaining but with praise to God turned out.

CHAPTER EIGHT

CONFESSION: LORD, I MESSED UP!

The Prayer of Confession is the prayer that acknowledges sin and wrong in a person's life. This prayer gets close to the heart of an individual. This is repenting and admitting to a fault or an unjust act which displeases God. Many categorize messing up as stealing, killing, lying, fornicating, and general immorality, but it is also disobeying and ignoring the voice and will of God. Anything that displeases God is sin, and sin messes us up.

A dear friend once shared a story concerning a straying relative. She was concerned about her son and was told that "everybody goes over fool's hill." And she responded, "I am afraid that he has gone over fool's hill and he's not coming back." It can be said of each of us that at some point in life, sin has taken us over fool's hill. Life appears many days to be filled with our messing up for one reason or another. It is evident that we have all messed up at some point, and whatever we find in our lives that will hurt or hinder our walk with God is messing us up.

Looking at the life of King David, we discover that even kings can mess up. David, according to 2 Samuel, committed adultery with another man's wife, Bathsheba, and had her husband, Uriah, murdered so he could marry her. No one knew what he had done, and as a king he thought he could not be touched. Nevertheless, God saw and knew everything and David was later confronted by the prophet Nathan. As a result of a powerful and prophetic confrontation, David was moved to write this prayer of confession. The story of King David in 2 Samuel 12-13 is a prime example of how David's sin caused him to be confronted, which brought him to pray a prayer of confession.

David's Prayer of Confession

Praying for Compassion

David recognizes that he is in need of compassion, which is God's tender love and forgiveness. He prays, "Have mercy on me, O God, because of your unfailing love.

Because of your great compassion, blot out the stain of my sins" (Psalm 51:1, NLT). He knows that he deserves justice, yet he knows the compassion of God will hide a multitude of sins. When we mess up, God's unfailing love is often seen in a generous way as we pray the prayer of confession. God's compassion is huge and large enough to wipe out our shortcomings. When we have fallen short with the sins in our lives, we must pray for God's mercy to be generous in our lives. We are moved to pray like David. After David had been confronted by the prophet Nathan, his attitude toward God and his sins changed. Therefore he prays not only for compassion, but he prays for cleansing.

Praying for Cleansing

This becomes another request as David repents and confesses his sins before the presence of God. David's prayer is for God to "Wash me clean from my guilt. Purify me from my sin" (Psalm 51:2, NLT). He prays for God to clean up not only his act, but his life. He requests a spiritual bath in order for his sins to be removed from his life. Confession aids in the cleansing of our sins. We are not able like David to cleanse ourselves, but we must rely on the Lord's help for cleansing. As our sins are revealed (and it is important that they are exposed and revealed for our own sakes), we can ask God to deliver us and cleanse us from the error of our ways. The prayer moves from cleansing to confession.

Praying for Confession

Here David prays to admit and acknowledge his sins. Notice the prayer language: "For I recognize my rebellion; it haunts me day and night. Against you, and you alone, have I sinned; I have done what is evil in your sight. You will be proved right in what you say, and your judgment against me is just" (Psalm 51:3-4, NLT). David does not pray to justify why he sinned; he just admits his wrong and pleads guilty to the error of his ways. He has missed the mark and repents of the sin in his life. We are often faced with the challenge of confessing our sins before God. Because David confesses, he agrees with God about the sin in his life. This allows God to meet us at our point of need. Our prayer fellowship and relationship with God can never reach its full potential if we don't confess our sins. Because David confesses, he recognizes his condition.

Praying for Condition

David now expresses his condition of being a sinner. He recognizes his state as an individual: "For I was born a sinner—yes, from the moment my mother conceived me.

But you desire honesty from the womb, teaching me wisdom even there" (Psalm 51:5-6, NLT).

David understands that his condition has been with him since birth and prays for new life so this condition will not interfere with his walk with God. When we learn of our sinful condition, it gives us the opportunity to pray for God to help us makes some changes in our lives. The help for our spiritual, selfish, and sinful conditions is found only in the Lord. Henceforth, we must pray like David for repair. His prayer moves from condition to repair.

Praying for Repair

As David acknowledges his condition, he seems to say to the Lord, "Fix me, Lord!" As one confesses after messing up, God needs to repair our sinful and broken lives. Note how David now prays in confession, "Purify me from my sins, and I will be clean; wash me, and I will be whiter than snow. Oh, give me back my joy again; you have broken me—now let me rejoice. Don't keep looking at my sins. Remove the stain of my guilt" (Psalm 51:7-9, NLT). David has lost his joy because of his sins. David needs fixing. He seems to be unhappy and uneasy because he has messed up with God more than with anyone else. Therefore, he wants God to fix him up again. He makes a request almost like a person, needing a car repaired in order to get to a job. He cannot be fully used again by God until his heart has been repaired and made over again. Sin can block the flow of the power of God in our lives, and whatever is blocking the flow must be fixed. David cannot be an effective king again until God fixes his life. David's prayer moves from return to renewal.

Praying for Renewal

As David continues to pray, his prayer is "Create in me a clean heart, O God" (Psalm 51:10a, NLT). He wants God to make him over again. He prays for a new and fresh start. He needs God to bring order back in his life. He has strayed and needs renewal. He prays for God to not only renew, but to revive his soul. The renewal comes through the breath of the Holy Spirit. David knows the danger Saul encountered playing and messing around with sin. The last thing he needs is a life without the presence of God. So in his renewal he prays, "Renew a loyal spirit within me" (Psalm 51:10b, NLT). This prayer of renewal is asking God not to abandon him because of his sins. Because sin separates us from God, confession will bring a time of renewal in our lives. We are often challenged to hide our sins, but it hurts our growth in the Lord. David understood the power of confession and how crucial it was for spiritual renewal and revival in our hearts. His confession moves from renewal to return.

Praying for Return

"Do not banish me from your presence, and don't take your Holy Spirit from me. Restore to me the joy of your salvation, and make me willing to obey you. Then I will teach your ways to rebels, and they will return to you" (Psalm 51:11-13, NLT). David recalls the joy he once had with God, but life after sin appears to be gloomy and gray. He needs a zeal that he once had for God. He no longer has the excitement of knowing God and prays for such emotion to return. He vows that once he is restored, he can testify and share with sinners their ungodly ways and likewise find a new life in God. What a wonderful way to confess. After acknowledging the wrong in our lives, we vow to God to help teach others about their wrongs so that God might fix them as well.

In summation David prays, "Yes, Lord, I've done wrong. I've messed up and I pray that you will clear the record. I am in a mess and you're the only one who can get me out." David was praying for a way out. David did not have an advocate. David did not have a lawyer to speak on his behalf. David did not have a middleman in his messed up situation to speak and plead his case. But thanks to God. When we've messed up, we can pray and be delivered because 1 John teaches us that "If any man sin, we have an advocate with the Father, Jesus Christ, the righteous and he is the propitiation for our sins and not for ours only, but for the sins of the whole world."

Prayer of Confession

Dear Lord, I admit to any wrong that I have done in my life. I confess that I have not been all I could have been to you and for you. There have been numerous times when I disobeyed you. I have fallen short of your will so many times. I ask you now Lord to forgive me for _____ (list sins or errors you wish to confess). Like David, I acknowledge my transgressions, sins, and iniquities. Father, I ask that you search my life and change my heart, my head and my hands, so that I may feel, think and do your will daily. I know that you died for my sins, and I pray that your blood will cover them. Help me, Lord, not to commit those same sins again. I am in desperate need of You and Your help, in the spirit of repentance and forgiveness I pray. Amen.

Study Questions

1. Why is the prayer of confession important in our lives?
2. What is the purpose of a prayer of confession?
3. How did twhis prayer affect the life of David? How does it affect your life?

4. Do you believe that David would have confessed his sins if Nathan had not confronted him? Why or Why not?

5. Why is it often difficult to confess our sins, publicly or privately?

Prayer Activity

Ask the Holy Spirit to reveal to you any areas of unconfessed sins in your life. Repent and thank God for His forgiveness. Read through the prayer above if necessary.

CHAPTER NINE

SUPPLICATION: PRAYING WHEN YOU ARE HAVING TROUBLE

The Prayer of Supplication has been the most known way to pray. For years, I thought this was the only way to pray. Before the teaching of adoration, confession, submission and other prayers, we were petitioning God on a regular basis for help in our times of need. The prayer of supplication is a prayer when we are in trouble or in a crisis. Crisis, suffering, and struggles often lead us to times of intense prayer. Supplication is approaching the throne of God in times of despair, distress, and discomfort. It is seeking God, as if one is on a spiritual campaign, making a plea for help. It's when we are in trouble in one form or another and none but God is able to help. The Prayer of Supplication is a prayer for a sickness that needs healing, a prayer in confusion that needs peace, a prayer in bondage that needs freedom, a prayer in sorrow that needs joy, and a prayer in darkness that needs light or just a prayer in troubled times that need some comfort. Whatever the trouble might be, it causes one to cry out to God.

Job noted that "Man that is born of a woman is of a few days and full of trouble" (Job 14:1). It is safe to note that in this life, we are going to have some trouble. At some point or another we will have some kind of trouble. Everybody has trouble sometimes. There are times when our son's teachers will issue them a homework pass, which exempts them from doing a homework assignment. Although schools offer exemptions from homework, life never exempts us from its troubles. There are no trouble-free passes in this life. We are either in trouble, going into trouble, or coming out of trouble. Life seems to be always associated with trouble of some kind. Perhaps the first stanza of Paul Lawrence Dunbar's poem, "Life," may speak to how we view life at times: "A crust of bread and a corner to sleep in, A minute to smile and an hour to weep in, A pint of joy to a peck of trouble, and never a laugh but the moans come double; and that is life!" In this life, we are going to have some trouble, but just because we are having trouble does not mean trouble should have us. God has given us a plan for handling the troubles of life. The Lord does have a way of saving us in the midst of the dangers we might be facing and experiencing in life.

King Hezekiah could have easily rendered this testimony because such was the case with him. Being a godly king, he walked close with the Lord. Nevertheless, one day King Hezekiah received a death notice from the prophet Isaiah to "set his house in order" because he had to die. There are several prayer lessons that we learn from King Hezekiah. We learn that in trouble we must turn, plead, and receive. We turn to God, we plead with God, and we receive from God.

We Turn to God

Hezekiah turns his face to the wall and begins to pray and weep. Hezekiah finds himself in a crisis, and he does not speak to doctors or medical professionals, but he speaks to the Lord. He is in need of help, and at the moment it could only come from God. King Hezekiah knew that his integrity and godly lifestyle would account for something with God. When we receive bad news as Hezekiah did, we are often tempted to panic. However, presenting our case to God helps us to release the stress and strain of the news. Psalm 55:22 encourages us to "Cast thy burdens on the

Lord and He shall sustain thee. He will not suffer the righteous to be moved" (KJV). Praying is the best way to release our troubles to God. It is a consolation to know that when we are really in tuned with God, God will not turn the volume down or off on our prayers, but He hears and responds.

We Plead with God

Hezekiah approaches God in humility. He says, "Remember, Now O Lord . . ."(NIV). Here, King Hezekiah wants to get a prayer through. He is intentional in his praying to God. There are times when the only person you can share your burdens with is God. Hezekiah is not trying to impress God; he's just trying to reach Him. Hezekiah does not pray a long prayer, but an effective prayer. Sometimes, "Lord, have mercy" or "Lord, help!" may be all you have at the time. Praying sincerely can get God's attention. On a regular basis we often have longer prayer time. However, when praying when you're in trouble, depending upon the situation, you do not always have time for a long prayer. No matter how difficult the situation may be, if the prayer is from the heart, it reaches God! Sometimes we have to pray and get some things off of us and place them in greater hands than ours. Who better to tell than God? He understands more than anyone else. Hezekiah released his problem into the hands of God, but he also needed to share some things on his heart with God. He remembers his walk with God. In one hundred years, Hezekiah was the only king whose character was in accordance with the will of God. Who Hezekiah was, was more important that what he did. Hezekiah was not boasting about walking upright before God, but he was in trouble and he needed to present some facts to support his petition.

We Receive from God

Before the Prophet Isaiah could leave the grounds of the palace, Hezekiah's prayer had already moved God to the point of action. "And it came to pass, afore Isaiah was gone out of the middle court, that the word of the Lord came to him, saying, Turn again, and tell Hezekiah that captain of my people, Thus saith the Lord, the God of David thy father, I have heard thy prayer, I have seen thy tears: behold, I will heal thee: on the third day thou shalt go up unto the house of the Lord" (2 Kings 20:4-5, KJV). It is certain that we pray to receive answers and directions from God. One of the benefits of praying is for the one who prays to get a prayer through and a response from God.

The word that Isaiah delivers to Hezekiah the second time from the Lord is "I will add unto thy days fifteen years; and I will deliver thee and this city out of the hand of the king of Assyria; and I will defend this city for mine own sake, and for my servant David's sake" (2 Kings 20:6, KJV). In response to Hezekiah's prayer, God not only heals his body and adds fifteen more years to his life, but he delivers him from the hands of his enemies. When God begins to move He has the power to handle more than one problem in our lives at a time! When we are in trouble—and it does not matter what kind of trouble it is—if we are honest with ourselves, we want to recover from the trouble. People trouble, church trouble, husband trouble, wife trouble, child trouble, preacher trouble, member trouble, money trouble, job trouble, heart trouble, stomach trouble, back trouble, head trouble, double trouble, and sometimes it will be trouble everywhere you look. Whatever the trouble is, we want to recover. The goal for the person who prays, in this instance, is deliverance and recovery from the trouble. After praying earnestly, Hezekiah recovered and lived fifteen more years. God honored the prayer of the righteous king.

The late Brother Elsie Horne, who was a faithful member of a church I pastored in North Carolina, then in his late seventies, gave a wonderful interpretation of how to know when God is answering one's prayers. He said, "Reverend, when you begin to pray and you begin to feel a tug in your soul and a good feeling of peace comes over you, then that lets you know that God is answering your prayer." What Mr. Horne was explaining was that when God has received our prayers, there is a sense of peace and contentment from having been in the presence of God. It's a joy to feel God tugging at your soul and giving signs that all is well! What we receive from God may not always be what we want, but it will always be what we need.

Maybe our trouble is not always as intense as Hezekiah's, and for others it could be more intense than Hezekiah's. Some may be faced with ruined health mentally, emotionally, physically, or spiritually. Perhaps bad news has set in on your life lately and you need a word of direction. Pray! Pray! Pray! Whatever the trouble—cancer, AIDS, heart disease, diabetes, arthritis, hypertension, or an addiction—it's a good case for God! Whatever your case or crisis, turn to the Lord in prayer. He's your friend and will meet you at your very point of need.

Disaster in our lives can often draw us closer to God through prayer. Recovery may not always be healing outwardly, but it is always healing inwardly. Recovery through prayer sometimes could be strength, direction, and wisdom to cope, handle, accept, and face the crisis that we are in. I have discovered that prayer is good for any and every situation in our lives.

We must know that when we are faced with trouble of any sort, we can pray. We can cry out to God. There is refuge in God! When we are tempted to run or rage, we can sit safely in God. When we are feeling lonely, prayer becomes a constant companion. When all else fails, in times of trouble, praying will make all the difference in the world. When we're in trouble, praying is not only the best thing to do, it is the right thing to do. God is able to meet us at our every point of need. Not only is God able, but He is willing. May we trust God enough to seek Him for guidance, strength, comfort, help, and safety! If trouble seems to be in your way, pray your way through it! We have a friend in Jesus who will help us, hold us, and strengthen us as we pray our way through trouble.

Prayer of Supplication

Help Lord! I have found myself in trouble. I don't know what to do, but I understand you know what to do. Father, if there is something I can do besides pray to make it through, please show me the way. If it is something that I cannot handle on my own, Lord, I give to permission to do what you do best, that is looking out for your children. Lord, these burdens appear to be more than I can handle, therefore, I ask you to help me these dark and difficult times of my life. I know that you are able, because you have come through so many times before, so Lord, here I am, at your mercy, praying for deliverance. Thanks for helping and thanks for listening. Lovingly Yours, your child. Amen. *(During this prayer time you may even want to state the troubles you are having).*

Study Questions:

1. Why do you believe we are more fervent crying out when we are in trouble than when we are not?

2. What made God respond to Hezekiah's prayer in such a swift time?

3. Can you think of a time in your life when God responded so swiftly? If so reflect upon and recall what your response was.

Prayer Activity:

If you are facing trouble, choose someone you know and trust to covenant with you to pray daily with you and for you during your times of trouble. A small prayer group would also be wonderful to assist you in praying through your times of crisis. It would also be appropriate for this area and season of your life, to sing, play, or quote the words from the hymn "I Need Thee Ev'ry Hour."

CHAPTER TEN

INTERCESSION: PRAYING FOR OTHER PEOPLE

ntercessory prayer is going to the throne of God on behalf of another. This area of prayer promotes growth in our prayer life because we are praying for people besides ourselves. The Prayer of Intercession is the time when we move beyond the needs of self and pray for the situations and needs of other people. It's like standing in the gap for another person. It is interceding on behalf of a brother, a sister, your spouse, your child(ren), parents, your pastor, your church member, your friends, and even your enemies. It is praying for people who may be too sick to pray for themselves or too heavily burdened to fight the spiritual battle alone. Thomas Merton, a monk at the Abbey of Gethesemani in

Trappist, Kentucky, was a person of constant prayer and deep spiritual thought. Merton believed greatly in intercessory prayer. Merton believed strongly in praying for others in their times of need and distress. He suggested that when the needs of others are prayed for, the person praying would also meet his or her own needs. It can be easily supposed for most of us that the prayers of others by God's grace have kept us alive, safe in danger, and going forward.

While it does not always makes sense to pray for others, praying for others keeps us from being selfish and always thinking our own problems. The ministry of intercession provides an opportunity to pray specifically for other people, ministries, and families by name. For example: A couple whose marriage is stormy, someone whose finances are unstable, someone who has wayward children, someone who is sick, someone who is unsaved, and someone who needs deliverance from a habit or a situation are opportunities to speak to God on their behalf. Praying this way helps us to have more care, concern, and compassion for other people and the struggles they may be experiencing.

Intercessory prayer also reminds us that we all need someone else to pray for us! No matter how much we pray for ourselves and for other people, we are in dire need of the prayers of others. One of the greatest assignments for the Christian is to follow the words of James 5:16a: "Confess your faults one to another, and pray for one another, that you may be healed . . ." (KJV). One of the greatest dynamics of prayer is when we know that there are others praying for us and going to the throne of God on our behalf.

In order to understand the practice of intercession, there are two biblical passages that we shall look at concerning praying for others. Although we should regularly pray for our leaders and people in our families, we should also pray regularly for our enemies and those who have hurt us, intentionally and unintentionally. We shall discuss in this chapter three areas of prayer: praying for those who have hurt you, praying for those who have helped you, and praying for your spouse and children. *(My wife, Jean, contributed to the area of praying for your spouse and children from the perspective of a wife and mother.)*

Praying for Those Who Have Hurt You

In Luke 23:34 we read about Jesus Christ hanging on the cross dying between two thieves. Jesus stops dying long enough to pray for those who had wronged Him. He prays, "Father, forgive them for they know not what they do" (KJV). This prayer is for

God to release, restore, and forgive those who have caused this punishment upon Jesus Christ. Of course, they really did not know what they were doing. They did not know that the death of Jesus Christ would be life for every Christian believer! Who does Jesus pray for? Jesus prays for the Roman soldiers, Pilate, Herod, and the religious leader of His day. He was also praying for us because He was dying for our sins.

We must understand that this is not always an easy prayer to pray. To pray for people who have wronged, abused, misused, talked about, and confused us can really be a difficult task. Although a challenge, if we walk in the path of Christ, even praying for our enemies will prove to benefit us more spiritually than we could ever imagine. One of the greatest lessons my grandmother taught me was to pray for and love even the most difficult person you meet. She would say, "You can't help what other people do; if they mistreat you, pray for them and the Lord will fix it." Grandmother Willia Mae lived long enough to know that Matthew 5:44-45 is good for intercession:

> But I say unto you, Love your enemies, bless them that curse you, do good to them that hate you, and pray for them which despitefully use you, and persecute you; That

you may be the children of your Father which is in heaven: for He maketh His sun to rise on the evil and on the good, and sendeth rain on the just and on the unjust. (KJV)

From this lesson we learn to pray for those who have hurt us whether it was intentional or not.

Praying for Those Who Have Helped Us

The next area of intercession is when we pray for those who have helped us! Although this is a much easier task, it is also necessary. To illustrate this subject matter the Apostle Peter has been placed in jail around Easter time for preaching Jesus Christ. Peter was kept in jail, and the church called a prayer meeting. They prayed for the one who had helped them in so many times past. This is not a difficult prayer to pray. In fact, I have no problems praying for people who have been nice to me. Most of us delight in praying for our friends. We have a greater passion to pray for those who have helped us much more than for those who have hurt us. This is naturally so because we feel a deeper appreciation for that person, that person's ministry, and the God whom that person represents.

Peter was in trouble, and it was time to bail him out. Money could not bail him out, negotiations would not bail him out, rioting would not bail him out, boycotting would not bail him out, "But prayer was made without ceasing of the church, unto God for him" (Acts 12:5, KJV). Here we find the church in intercessory prayer: not praying for themselves, but for their leader, the Apostle Peter. Peter had prayed for them, and now it was no less than godly that someone would pray for Peter. Peter needed the church to come together and intercede to God on his behalf. Pastors and church leaders need prayer like anyone else does. This text teaches us that we must not only pray for sinners, but we must pray for the saints. The Lord sent an angel and miraculously delivered Peter from the prison cell, all because of some faithful Christians prayed without ceasing, purposefully, and diligently for Peter. This was not the first time Peter had someone to intercede on his behalf. Luke 22:31-32 prompts us to remember the words of Jesus: "Simon, Simon, behold, Satan hath desired to have you, that he may sift you as wheat: *but I have prayed for you*, that thy faith fail not: and when thou art converted, strengthen thy brethren" (KJV, emphasis mine).

Jesus teaches us here another dynamic of prayer. As Christian leaders, we are to pray for those who not only help us, but also for those who oppose, ridicule, resist, and reject our leadership, and what we are attempting to do to move the ministry forward. It is a known fact that when we are in leadership, those who follow have a better notion on how to get it done. Nevertheless, as they criticize, murmur, and complain, we must offer them up to God rather than making an effort to do it our way.

Praying for Our Families

Intercession from a Wife and Mother's Heart, by Jean McMurray Leake

Interceding for Husband

"At the dawn of a new marriage, twenty years ago, my aim was to be a good wife for Eric, in my own strength. Praying for him without ceasing was a privilege. It was something I did without thinking. As days grew in the marriage and ministry, challenges came upon us that we often did not know how to handle. There were many days my soul and spirit would wrestle. The temptation was to sleep through the conflicting and difficult times. However, I came to discover that you cannot sleep trouble away, fight trouble away, or even argue trouble away. There were even days I wondered if we could pray trouble away, encountering the kind of warfare from being married to a man after God's heart.

Once I discovered my gift of discernment and call to intercession, I began to ask God to direct me in how I could help with the ministry and begin flowing in His anointing. What we come to discover is that God shows us how to pray for one another as we learn this is not about us, but what God is assigning us to do. It is a joy to know that God has chosen me to be the wife of a man who reminds me of Job, a man always wanting to please God and never saying anything against God. Even when money was gone, even after losing a baby and making sacrifices, he stayed unshakeable. I have watched God take this man and grow him up to be a servant through the power of prayer. When we pray and ask God to bless our husbands, we are also allowing God to bless us too! (*Remember, the two shall become one).* May I encourage spouses to pray for each other daily! Pray for their strength and God's strength in them. Pray for their protection and for God to deliver them from any struggles, stress, and strain that often come with just being human. Praying for our spouses will help us draw closer to them and to God!

Interceding for Children

Being a mother is one of the toughest jobs one could ever love. I learned how to pray for my children through praying for other people's children. The Lord has blessed us with four children: one daughter and three sons. Because of our past lives, we knew how to pray for them to break the generational curses that we struggled with in the past. As our children grew (and are growing) and became involved in circles outside of the home, my prayer life increased for them. We are learning to pray for them, their schools, their community, and their church. This motivated me to pray bad stigmas away from them so that the will of God would take care of their lives and not what other people spoke against them outside of the will of God. I pray favor and wisdom upon our children and for God to surround them with positive speaking people, who speak life over them and not death, doom, or devastation.

God often uses our children to keep us humble and in the posture of prayer. As children grow they begin to develop their own personalities, goals, dreams, and attitudes. While the teenage years are often difficult, they increase the calling of intercession in a parent's life.

So through prayer, God has led me to consider myself a career woman! My career and ministry is working and praying for my husband and interceding for our children with the help of the Holy Spirit as He works through my body, mind, soul, and spirit.

Praying for your children never means that they will always be perfect, make decisions you agree with, and fully follow God's will—until they are willing to do so themselves. However, praying for them gives God the permission to begin to influence their ways so that when they come to a place of decision for God and to please Him, the way has been set through our prayers. All of our children have areas of struggle, just as we do, and taking those areas of need to God for our children can make all the difference in where they end up. The evil forces are out to destroy our children and will even use the mouths of other believers to speak evil and doom on them. Nevertheless, God calls us to stand in the gap for our children. When we cannot lead our children, go with our children, or even help our children, we can always pray for our children. When we do not understand our children, we can pray for our children. Just as my momma always did and still does pray for me, I pray for my children. Praying for our children places them in more capable hands than our own. After all, our children belong to God! May I encourage you to continue in prayer for your children"

The challenge for the body of Christ is to pray daily for one another and our partners in ministry. Growing up in a rural town—Mount Gilead, North Carolina—there was a song we used to sing. It was very simple but profound: "You pray for me and I'll pray for you, that's the way we Christians do." Praying for others does not only bless those who are being prayed for, but it blesses the person who is doing the praying. I see intercessory prayer as a win-win situation. As God meets the needs of others, He meets those who are doing the praying! May we never forget that the greatest intercession is constantly going on by Jesus Christ according to Romans 8:34. This is a word of consolation! While we are praying for others, someone is praying for us, but most importantly, Jesus Christ is interceding at this very moment for all of us! Thanks be to God for the gift, power, and ministry of intercessory prayer! May we trust God enough to pray for others, as His son, Jesus Christ, prays for us!

Prayer for Intercession

Dear Lord, I pray that I will be more diligent in praying for other people in my life. I pray that you would help me to learn to release the burdens of others to you in prayer. I ask, Father, that you would help me to know the difference between interceding and intervening. May I know when to pray for others and when to step in and help someone who may be in need. May I be a faithful intercessor in praying not only for those who have hurt me and those who help me, but also the lost, the poor, the needy, my family, my pastor, my congregation, and my community. This I ask in Jesus' name. Amen.

Study Questions:

1. How does the prayer of forgiveness Jesus prayed in this chapter relate to your life?

2. Is it difficult for you to pray for people who have hurt you? Why?

3. What is the difference to you in praying for people who have hurt you and praying for people who have helped you?

4. How does praying for someone else, benefit us?

Prayer Application and Activity:

Praying for Those Who Have Hurt You

(Intercessory Prayer #1)

Dear Lord, I have been having a hard time lately with _____ (name the person). I have not been able to concentrate on spiritual things because I have been focusing on my enemies rather than on you. Lord, I want to pray right now for my enemies, that you will help them, not to leave me alone, but to please you. I pray that he/she will make you Lord over his/her life. *(If she/he makes you Lord over her/his life, they won't mistreat me because of their love for you.)* I pray that you will find a way to bless them, and whatever causes them to hurt other people, please move it from them, so that he/she can live a victorious life in You. I pray blessings and not curses upon my enemy so that You can get the glory out of their lives. Bless their walk, their job, their family so that they will have abundant living, in Your Name I pray. Amen. *(Note: Consider writing on a separate sheet of paper who hurt you, how they hurt you, and then practice praying for them and choosing to forgive them. Then tear it up!)*

Praying for Those Who Have Helped You (Intercessory Prayer #2)

Dear Father, I come now to stand in the gap for _____. I pray for her/him as they face_____. I ask dear Lord that you help _____ (name of person) in these difficult times. They need your help at this hour. They are confronted with some real struggles these days and need your guidance. I pray that she/he will have peace in doing Your will and pleasing You in life and ministry. Lord, _____ *(Name the person)* is having some major spiritual battles these days and cannot seem to come out of them. Only you can help him/her come out of this battle. Lord whatever you want _____ to learn during this time; please reveal it to them so that _____ can grow to be the person you are calling for your service and in your kingdom. In the Spirit of Love for You and others, I pray. Amen.

Praying For Your Spouse (Intercessory Prayer #3)

Write down areas of concern for your husband or wife and pray them daily. Write down the areas of strength for your spouse and ask God to continue to bless them. Pray for your marriage and the blessings of God to be upon your marriage on a regular basis.

Praying For Your Children (Intercessory Prayer #4)

List the needs and challenges of your children and offer them up to God daily. Pray for your children's relationship with God and that they will live out their God-ordained potential. Pray for their present and their future. Keep a journal on each child and as you pray, and watch how God guides.

(You may also want to substitute words to pray for a congregation, pastor, or a ministry that is thriving or struggling).

CHAPTER ELEVEN

POWER THROUGH PRAYER AND FASTING!

——◦◦◦——

*W*hile the power of prayer is a dynamic force in an individual's life, prayer and fasting together make a greater force for growth, guidance, deliverance and Christian maturity. Throughout the scriptures we can truly see the powerful effects of prayer and fasting. Fasting is when we deprive the physical to strengthen the spiritual. People fast for different reasons: Some fast for health purposes or to cleanse their bodies, and others have fasted to God for miracles, repentance, spiritual renewal, and to bring the flesh under control. According to the Lord Jesus, there are some miracles we will never see without prayer and fasting (Mark 9:29). Fasting and prayer go hand in hand. The two are not to be separated because one provides spiritual reinforce-ment to the other.

Fasting is a spiritual discipline that provides insight that one would not receive just by doing ordinary things. John Wesley, the founder of the Methodist Movement, was such a strong believer in fasting that he refused to ordain any preacher who did not agree to fasting at least twice a week. In most cases, fasting is a very private matter. However, there are times when fasting is corporate with a group of people for a specific purpose or need. Fasting is a sacrifice; it is submission and spiritual service to God.

As a sacrifice, fasting is an act of surrendering one's flesh for a greater cause. This part of fasting is the offering up of the flesh to hear clearly from God. We give up what we like, want, and need as an act of faith.

As submission we are yielding. When we fast, things often change or slow down. As we change our eating habits, we also change our schedules and lifestyles to connect totally with God. Therefore, fasting is an act of humility. As we submit to the voice, will, and word of God, we will experience peace and purpose for our lives.

Fasting can also be viewed as an act of service. Service in this case is the offering of self to God through obedience. I have discovered that whenever I have fasted, no matter the time or the reason; I have always gotten clear direction from God. Therefore, fasting has provided direction for ministry. Fasting can also help us do a greater job in the work of ministry because it provides strength and power to do ministry. Paul writes to the Romans, "Present your bodies a living sacrifice, holy, acceptable unto God which is your reasonable service" (Romans 12:1b, KJV).

In this chapter you will find the purpose, principles, and practice of fasting. We shall view fasting in the Old and New Testament. We shall discuss various types of fast, what to do and what not to do when fasting, as well as some helpful hints on the fasting journey. The attitude, posture, and power of fasting are also included in this chapter to help those who are new to fasting understand what God's purpose and design for fasting is in your life or ministry.

The Purpose of Fasting

"Is not this the fast that I have chosen? To loose the bands of wickedness, to undo The heavy burdens, and to let the oppressed go free, and that ye break every

yoke? is it not to deal thy bread to the hungry, and that thou bring the poor that are cast out to thy house? When thou seest the naked, that thou cover him; and that thou hide not thyself from thine own flesh? Then shall thy light break forth as the morning, and thine health spring forth speedily: and thy righteousness shall go before thee: the glory of the Lord shall be thy reward." (Isaiah 58: 7-8, KJV).

According to Isaiah 58, there are some powerful dynamics that cannot be ignored as relates to fasting. These verses teach us why we should fast and how it should be done. Isaiah speaks of God's chosen fast for His people. The purposes of fasting are to loose the chains of injustice, untie the chords of the yoke, set the oppressed free, break every yoke, feed the hungry, shelter the homeless, clothe the naked, and experience spiritual renewal and deliverance from the Lord. The design of fasting then is to help set others and ourselves free from fleshy and spiritual bondage, but also to meet the needs of the poor, needy, and oppressed that we are surrounded by daily. Fasting reminds us to give up what is common to us and to watch God do the uncommon in our lives. These verses teach us that when we fast God's way, supernatural strength is given to individuals and groups who trust God with such sacrifice. True, sincere fasting brings light, life, good health, and righteousness, and God's glory will shine all about us as a result of true, sincere fasting. God moves in marvelous and awesome ways when we engage in His chosen fast. It challenges us to not only meet our spiritual needs but the spiritual and physical needs of others also. What a wonderful opportunity for ministry through a sacrifice such as fasting!

The Principles of Fasting

"Moreover, when you fast, be not, as the hypocrites, of a sad countenance: for they appear unto men to fast. Verily I say unto you, they have their reward. but thou, when thou fastest, anoint thine head, and wash thy face; that thou appear not unto men to fast, but unto thy Father which is in secret: and thy Father, which seeth in secret, shall reward thee openly." Matthew 6:16-18 (KJV).

Matthew 6:16-18 teaches us the principles and posture of fasting. We are taught that there is an attitude for fasting as there is for prayer and giving in the previous verses of Matthew 6. We are admonished to fast for the right reasons, not for a show or compliment from people; we must fast unto God. We should not look for the praise of people or openly broadcast that we are fasting. We should not look sad so that it might draw attention to ourselves. The focus when fasting should be on God and not us. We should fast with great hope and expectations, anticipating mighty results from God!

It is also wise when fasting to pray often for others, the needs of the church, or other ministries—for personal growth, guidance, and direction from the Lord. The Father who sees in secret will reward openly. When we are fasting and going without food, we should feed off of the word of God. God's word can give us spiritual strength in times of physical weakness.

The Practice of Fasting

Fasting can be corporate or private. Below are several places in the Old and New Testament where God moved in people's lives as a result of prayer and fasting. Many lives were transformed through prayer and fasting. Some nations were delivered from bondage and even judgment through sincere prayer and fasting. The following areas are places in the Old and New Testaments that teach about prayer and fasting and some results of what took place in their lives. These verses can be used for personal and public study to enhance and understand the practice of biblical fasting:

The Practice of Fasting in the Old Testament

- Moses—Exodus 34:28 (Private)

- Elijah—I Kings 19:8 (Private)

- Judah—II Chronicles 20:3-12 (Corporate)

- Nehemiah—Nehemiah 1:3-11 (Private)

- Daniel—Daniel 10:3 (Private)

- Nineveh—Jonah 3:4-10 (Corporate)

- A Call to Fast—Joel Chapter 2 (Corporate)

The Practice of Fasting In the New Testament

- Matthew 6:16-18

- Anna—Luke 2:37 (Private)

- Jesus—Luke 4 and Matthew 4

- Paul—Acts 9:9

- Cornelius—Acts 10:30-31

- Church at Antioch—Acts 13:2

The Practice of Fasting Today

There are numerous ways people have fasted in these modern times. Typically fasting is without food. Some have gone without television, harsh words, shopping, and other things that perhaps are harmful to us in some way. However, what I shall provide are ways I believe people can fast and experience a movement of God in life and ministry. We shall discuss the ultimate fast, the water fast, the juice fast, and the Daniel Fast. I shall also provide some helpful tips about fasting, the length of your fast, and some fasting suggestions for those who cannot participate in an ultimate fast for one reason or another.

The Ultimate Fast

The Ultimate Fast, which is found in Exodus 34:27-28, is the fast that Moses did in Exodus and Jesus Christ did in the New Testament (Matthew 4:1-2; Luke 4:1-2). These are extremely miraculous fasts because typically the longest a person can go without water is about three days before becoming dehydrated. This type of fast is supernatural. This implies that only God can carry and sustain an individual through such times. Some people I know have gone two to five days without anything but found it very difficult and challenging to their body. Despite those challenges, they have also testified that they saw the mighty hand of God move in their lives.

The Water Fast

The water fast is, of course, water only! This is when one eats no food but takes in water to keep from getting dehydrated. Persons who feel led to this type of fast should consult a Christian physician for guidance, direction, and confirmation. This type of fast can be very difficult on a person who does a lot of hard labor. Because fasting is an act of faith, if this is what the Holy Spirit is leading you to do, you want to be careful and sensitive enough to obey the voice of the Holy Spirit in your life. Obedience is the key to fasting.

The Juice Fast

This is the fast most common for me. For persons who have health challenges and need a little more to sustain them, the Holy Spirit works just as powerful in a juice fast as He will in any other fast. Let us remember that what's important is our obedience to what the Lord is directing us to do. The juice fast is juice and water. One can have diluted fruit juices, vegetable juices, and broth from vegetables (boil vegetables and drink the broth from the vegetables). Some even take fruit and vegetable smoothies during a fast. This gives the body nutrients despite not partaking of solid food.

The Daniel Fast

This fast has often been referred to as the "Wisdom Fast" or the "Daniel Diet" (Daniel 1:15, 17). The Daniel Fast can also be found in Daniel 10:3. Daniel noted that for three weeks (twenty-one days), he ate no bread or meat, drank no wine, and used no fragrant oils. Like any other fast, this type of fast requires prayer and making adjustments in one's eating habits. All fasts, when they are done properly, have not only spiritual benefits but also physical benefits. Not eating or making adjustments in our eating can often give our bodies a rest from digesting the hard foods that we eat, such as meat and processed foods. This fast is without meat, bread, sugar drinks, and sweets. It is eating only what has been grown out of the ground. This would be fruit, vegetables, nuts, dried beans, fruit juices, and water. The result of Daniel fasting was that he received wisdom and understanding for dreams and visions (Daniel 1:17), his spiritual and physical countenance was renewed (Daniel 1:15), and his prayers were answered with understanding (Daniel 10:12). For those who are not accustomed to fasting, this is a good place to begin a new journey with the discipline of fasting.

Suggested Ways to Fast

I have discovered that fasting is new to a lot of people and must be approached with wisdom, sincerity, faith, and reverence to God. Following are some practical ways to fast. I believe that no Christian has been left with an excuse when it comes to fasting because even it one must eat, there are certain fasts that will allow us to do that so that we can all experience breakthroughs in our lives. I especially want to encourage persons who have not tried fasting (except for surgery or a doctor's appointment) to pray about what type of fast the Lord would have you do.

Fasting Suggestions

✝ Twelve-Hour Fast for a certain number of days. One could do a twelve-hour fast without eating or drinking for three, five, seven, twelve, twenty-one, or even forty days. You are still partaking of food, but only at certain times of the day. This helps one to be extremely disciplined, especially when one is at an eating function and is in a time of fasting.

✝ Do a seven-, twelve-, twenty-one-, or forty-day Daniel Fast. This is a fast in which you choose certain foods and abstain from the meats, bread, sugar drinks, and sweets. It is changing your diet and getting on God's agenda. It is a fast with fruit, vegetables, nuts, juice, and water.

✝ Fast one day a week. A twenty-four–hour fast can be just as powerful as others when it is done out of faith and obedience. On this fast you could probably go twenty-four hours without water, juice, and food. Activities will have to be limited, but God will sustain you.

✞ Do a three- to seven-day juice-only fast. With this fast you want to be careful to drink plenty of water. Activity on this fast also needs to be limited. Juices, water, and vegetable broth will provide a good source of energy and renewal for the spiritual, physical, and mental part of the individual.

✞ Fasting can also become a lifestyle for the Christian. There are many Christians who select a certain day of the week for fasting in some form or another. Many Methodist Christians around the world practice what they call the "Wesleyan Fast." This fast begins after the Thursday Evening meal and goes until mid-afternoon on Friday. It becomes a sacrifice and a weekly spiritual discipline as well.

Preparing for a Fast

Begin preparing your body for fasting several days before the fast, if possible. Occasionally, God may lead you on a personal fast in a day. Pray and select the number of days you feel God leading you to fast. If the Lord leads you to go a day without food, follow His leading! Drink lots of water or unsweetened juices (not much orange juice: acids may be harmful on an empty stomach).

Freshly Squeezed Lemon Juice in Water or diluted Apple Juice can also serve as a cleanser for the body.

Breaking a Fast

Breaking a fast is just as important as beginning a fast. Avoid spicy and fried foods. Eat raw fruit and vegetables if you have gone several days without solid food. Slowly move to steam vegetables and in a week or so begin to incorporate regular food into your diet.

Prayer and Fasting

While you are on the fast, it is extremely important that you partake of spiritual disciplines. The reading and study of the scripture and prayer are crucial. These become our nourishment while not eating physical food or abstaining from certain foods. For example, if you are working on a job while fasting, when lunch time comes, rather than joining others for lunch, go to a quiet place, pray and read the Bible, use your journal, and sense what the Holy Spirit is speaking to you. Effective fasting must be done through prayer and the word of God.

Personally, I have watched God transform the lives of others and my life and provide miracles in my family, in a congregation, and a ministry as a result of fasting. Fasting is not always an easy service to perform, especially in this age and country of plenty. Yet those who are willing to participate in fasting on a regular basis will begin to see powerful results in the struggling areas of their lives.

I am thankful for this discipline of fasting. It has provided spiritual strength for a spiritual journey in a fleshy body. Fasting teaches us that we can deny ourselves in a good way and receive spiritual blessings in the process. I encourage you to try it. There are enough creative ways to let it happen and be blessed!

Prayer for Fasting: Pray This Prayer before Fasting

Dear Lord, I ask that you would guide and direct me in fasting. I am well aware that fasting is a part of your will for every believer. I also know that there are some things that I will never overcome with a lifestyle of prayer and fasting. Please show me how you would have me to fast, what to fast for, and the length of the fast. I desire to be totally sold out to you. Please help me to understand the practice, the principles, the purpose, and the power of fasting. I am willing to make the necessary adjustments, so Lord please help me to take this giant leap of faith in my life for you. In Jesus' Name. Amen!

Study Questions:

1. Why is fasting an important discipline for the Christian?

2. What is the purpose of fasting?

3. Have you ever fasted before? What were the results?

4. Why do you believe people in the bible were victorious when they fasted?

Prayer and Fasting Activity:

Prayerfully choose a time of fasting.

1. Write in a journal why you are fasting, the type of fast you are doing, and the length of your fast.

2. Pray before you begin the fast, pray throughout the fast, and pray at the end of the fast.

3. Activities should be reduced as much as possible so as not to overload the body during a time of fasting.

4. Write down what you sense the Lord is doing and anything that may be different (emotions, thoughts, etc.).

5. Take note of the difficult times as well as times of breakthroughs.

6. Trust the Holy Spirit to carry you through the challenging moments of going without food or certain foods.

How to Journal

For personal and spiritual growth, you are encouraged to do the following for journaling:

1. As you pray and read the scriptures, be aware of what you sense and a prompting or leading from the Holy Spirit.

2. Write what you sense is taking place, such as where you are, what is going on around you, who is present, and how you are responding.

3. Write the kinds of prayers you have prayed.

4. Record certain things that have been said to you by others.

5. Write what you have discovered about yourself on your daily journey.

6. Pour yourself out to God and see how you have grown spiritually.

7. Be open and honest so that the Holy Spirit can work in and through you!

CHAPTER TWELVE

THE GOD WHO ANSWERS BY FIRE!

*s previously stated, when we pray we expect a response or an answer from God. While we believe that God does answer our prayers, He often has a strange way of answering them. We have discovered that He can even answer our prayers through fire. Fire: what an unusual way to answer prayer! All throughout the scriptures God has shown up in fire. Fire represents the presence of God. When the Israelites were in the wilderness, God was a cloud of smoke by day and a pillar of fire by night (Exodus 13:21). We need fire to keep warm, but we also need fire to give us light. Although fire burns and destroys wood, hay, paper, and other things, fire will also purify gold and refine silver. Fire is important to sustain life. If fire is that important to life, how much more important is fire for those who follow God and serve in ministry? If we need fire (heat) in the winter time and fire to burn light and fire in our engines to transport us, we need fire in our hearts, in our lives, in our churches, and in our communities.

When we speak of fire, we are referring in this context to fresh encounters with God. This is what keeps prayer exciting. When we pray, we expect God to show up, although we are not always aware of how He will show up. This gives those who earnestly pray a spirit of expectation and anticipation when we pray. We should have the expectation that God will do something different, fresh, unusual, and unprecedented in our lives. When God shows up, He shows up in purposeful and powerful ways! When God answers by fire, He does things we have never seen Him do before. God keeps things fresh because if He keeps doing the same things over and over, we would begin to worship what God is doing and has done rather than worshipping God. There are occasions God has to send us fresh fire so that we might live like burning bushes, which burn without burning up (Exodus 3). I have no doubt that the fire of God has not totally gone from the people of God! As God continues to answer prayer, I truly believe that we can expect the fire of God to fall. When I speak of fire, I speak of that which is out of the ordinary, when God breaks through our lives and even public worship services with a movement that shifts the worship celebration and causes transformation in the hearts and minds of those present.

It is God's will that the souls of His people would catch on fire with His presence and His power! What a mighty revival would break out and change the atmosphere around us. I would hasten to advocate that the church does not need any spiritual "fire fighters," or those who will water down prayer and the power of God, but those who will be instruments of igniting a heavenly fire through the practice and power of prayer. Organization is wonderful, mobilization is good, strategizing is crucial, and networking is essential, but unless these are bathed in prayer and ignited with the fire of God, they will be short lived.

We can learn this lesson from the Prophet Elijah on Mount Carmel (1 Kings 18). Elijah helps us to realize what happens when power and prayer meet even when the odds are stacked against us. Elijah finds himself in a contest on Mount Carmel with the Israelites and the Prophets of Baal. This prophet has encountered some extraordinary miracles through the power of God. He speaks and there is no rain for three-and-a-half years because he speaks the word. Ravens brought him bread and meat in the morning and bread and meat in the evenings, and he drank water from the brook. One day the brook dried up and the raven didn't come, and he went one hundred miles down the road to Zarephath and a widow fed him, her son, and herself three-and-a-half years. Her son died, and he brought him back to life. But now he is confronted with a more intense matter. He is faced with Jezebel the controlling queen and Ahab the King. They were in charge of 450 prophets that worship Baal and 400 prophets of the groves, all of which ate at Jezebel's table. They worshipped Baal, who was the god of "dew and fertility." Elijah calls the people of Israel into account, "How long halt ye, between two opinions" (1 Kings 18:21, KJV), meaning how long will you keep jumping from one God to another god? They went from a little god to a big god! To halt is to falter, limp, hop, dance, or leap. He is asking them how long will you keep on dancing from one leg to the other? Their opinions were about trying to worship God and Baal at the same time. They wanted both YAHWEH and Baal and you can't have both. Could that be what often hinders the fire of God in our lives and our churches today? Are we dancing back and forth from the ways of God to the ways of the world? It seems that we want our way and God's way or the world's way and God's way and we can't have both. What we find here is a contest between "good and evil," "right and wrong," "light and darkness," "hot and cold." Elijah comes up with a grand idea, why don't we both pray to our God. You pray to your god and I will pray to my God and the God who answers by fire, He is God! The people agreed with the Prophet's proposal.

Elijah gave the Israelites all day to call on Baal. They kept calling on Baal. They called on Baal all day long, but there was no fire and no answers. They kept calling him and Baal would not answer. Elijah began to make fun of them and began to suggest "maybe he's on vacation, maybe he's on an errand, call him a little louder, maybe he's asleep and you need to wake him up." They prayed and prophesied until evening, but no answer came and no voice from Baal was heard. This is the disappointment of putting faith and hope in something or someone who is not able to deliver or respond when we call. It's like pleading or praying to one who does not have the same ability or availability as God does. As Elijah waits his turn to prove the True and Living God, he takes spiritual authority that God has given him. We begin to see what happens when God answers by fire. When God answers by fire, He answers with prayer, with power, and with presence. What a mighty work of God we witness when God answers by fire!

The God Who Answers By Fire, Answers with Prayer-verses 36-37

We see in verses 36-37 of this chapter that Elijah knew who to call, and he knew it would not take all day for Him to answer. Elijah prayed for the Lord to let it be known that He was God and that he was God's servant, who acted at God's command. He prayed for the Lord to answer him in a way that would turn the people's hearts back to God. Elijah was a man of prayer. If he prayed and the heavens shut up from rain and he prayed three-and-a-half years later and it rained again, how much more could he expect to pray for fire and it would come? Because of Elijah's obedience to God he was able to pray and expect God to act on his behalf! Fred Hartley in his book *Prayer on Fire* writes, "Prayer is what we do. It is our initiative to meet God, whether we are asking for favors, singing in celebration, or crying out in distress. Regardless of what shape or size it comes in, prayer is our effort to engage God. Fire on the other hand, is what God does. It is God's initiative to meet us."[7] If we want fire in our lives, we must pray for it; if we want fire back in our marriage, we must pray for it. If we want fire in the church, we must pray for it. If we want fire in the ministry, God has assigned us to pray for it because the only way God will send fire is that we pray for it. If the spark and

---

[7] Hartley, Fred. *Prayer on Fire* (Navpress: Colorado Springs, CO, 2006), 15.

fire of God is going to come back into our situations, it will come through prayer. Every move of God that the world has ever known has come through a prayer meeting.

I grew up in rural North Carolina. One of the ways we kept warm was with a wood heater. It was my responsibility to make sure there was always wood in the house so that we could keep warm in the winter. Each morning my mother would rise first. She would prepare breakfast and add wood to the fire or start a fresh fire if it had gone out throughout the night. One evening I decided that I would no longer get wood in because I was tired of doing it, and I went to bed. Early that cold winter morning, Mama got up to make a fire and there was no wood. Now let me tell you, even though there was no fire in the heater, there was heat in the house! Trust me when I tell you that the heat was on! Mama being the strict disciplinarian that she was; immediately stepped into my room (which was the closest room to the heater) and said, "Get up and go get some wood! I told you to get wood in yesterday and you didn't, now just get up and get out there and bring it in so I can make a fire!" This seemed to have been the coldest morning all winter, or at least it felt like it. Without a word uttered, I got up. However, I was probably boiling enough on the inside to warm up the whole house. I went to the wood pile and brought the wood inside. That afternoon, when I came home from school, I filled the back porch with wood from the bottom to the top. I wanted to make sure there was enough wood to last for a few days. What I later discovered was that if wood is what kept the fire burning and going, it did not only benefit me, but everyone in the house. When there is no wood for the fire, there can be no heat and if there is no heat, there is the lack of warmth and fire among us. Thus, when there is no wood (prayer) for the spiritual fire, the spiritual fire goes out. Prayer is wood that keeps the fire burning. We need more prayer warriors and churches as prayer centers, putting wood on the fire to keep the altars of God burning. We need God to raise up people and churches who will go back to putting wood on the fire so that the fire of God can continue to burn in a cold world! Let the fire of God fall and may the God who answers by fire answer through prayer. Let us pray until God returns in a noticeable way to our churches and our lives! We need some fire; a fire will always gather a crowd. Have you ever noticed what happens in a neighborhood when a fire breaks out? It draws people to the place where the fire is. They see the smoke, they perhaps hear a noise, and then they make their way to where the fire is. If we build a fire on the altar of prayer for God, not only will He come, but people will come as well. A meeting with God will bring the fire. Let us pray in our lives, in our homes, in our churches, and even in our communities and cities until the fire of God falls! We must pray until God answers by fire! God answers by fire through purposeful and sincere praying.

The God Who Answers By Fire, Answers With Power

Verse 38 tells that the power of God came down and moved in the midst of the people! God answered with power, and the power was manifested in the form of fire. Yet, the fire came as an answer or response to prayer. Erwin McManus wrote, "Sometimes we forget that God is fire, we confuse Him with fireplaces and fireworks." God is so much more powerful than fireplaces, fireworks, gas grills, gas ovens, boilers, furnaces, and heat pumps. God is a consuming fire (Hebrews 12:29, KJV). God sends fire to give us a glimpse of His character, His activity, His purposes, His power, and His presence. He sends fire to remind us that He is still in charge and will not share His glory with anyone. He answers with power: Everything moves by the power of God. God sent the fire, and the fire consumed the sacrifice, the stones, the dust, the wood, and the water in the trenches. They experienced awesome supernatural power of God in the form of fire! God answered with power, and the power was manifested in the form of fire. He sends fire to remind us that He is still in charge and will not share His glory with anybody. Miracles still take place when God's people pray! God sent the fire, and the people began to worship God! They proclaimed the Lord is God! He is still setting people on fire. He is the God, who answers by fire, but He answers with prayer, and He answers with Power.

As a pastor, I am often concerned about what we call worship void of the power and presence of God. It appears that what we call worship is our own selfish notions and rituals that make us feel good about ourselves without giving any consideration to whether or not God is pleased with our present worship experience. Lest I become misunderstood by these statements, let me be clear: the components of worship are not the issues. The issue is that we can easily control the components of worship until, if the Holy Spirit wanted to break through, He could not because He has in many churches been crowded out by the norm or the status quo of worship. Unless we become open to the direction of the Holy Spirit in our public worship settings, we will continue to experience decline in attendance, resources, but most of all in miracles. What's the solution? Prayer and fire! As the people of God pray sincerely and earnestly, we will begin once again to see the fire of God fall upon us! I'm not speaking here of religious activity, but the people of God in every generation praying and worshipping and trusting in a living God who brings fire in the midst of a cold, dull, and lifeless situation.

If there is going to be effectiveness and growth in our lives, it must come through prayer, but when we pray, we should look for God to respond with fire! The Lord still answers prayer. We expect God to show up with a manifestation of His supernatural presence. This makes all the difference in the world in our praying. If the darkness around us going to be removed and the light of Jesus Christ is going to invade the darkness in our hearts and society, then prayer must be the main thing on the Christian's agenda.

Let us remain steadfast in calling upon the one true God, Jehovah, who answers by fire. Yes, He does answer through prayer, power, and presence. What miracles the church could experience if we earnestly prayed for the fire of God to fall!

The God Who Answers By Fire, Answers With Presence-39

When Elijah prayed, the power of God came, and when the power of God came, it was evident that God was in their midst. As a result of the presence of God they began to worship God. True prayer brings not just the power of God, but the presence of God. The response from the people was worship. The presence of God filled the air where they were. They proclaimed the Lord is God! They recognized that they we were in the presence of God. God showed up in the form of fire! What the Israelites experienced that day was the presence and glory of God like they had never witnessed before. We know that God is everywhere, but there are times when He reveals Himself in our midst. Omnipresence means God is everywhere; manifest presence means God is here. He sits with us, and He lets us know that He has shown up. That's the God of fire and the God who answers by fire. When God manifest Himself, he brings with Him everything we need for the time. These Israelites needed to be brought back to reality of who the real and true God was. He showed up by fire, and they knew the presence of the Lord was there. He showed up in the atmosphere. You know when the Lord shows up, and you know when the Lord has not shown up. You cannot manufacture the presence of God, mimic the presence of God, or manipulate the presence of God. Only God can bring Himself into a situation. But His presence will change the atmosphere. When we talk about fire, what we are really talking about is God's presence; in His presence is fullness of joy and His right hand are pleasures forevermore (Psalm 16:11, KJV). Would to God that the His fire and His power would rest upon us in such a way that we experience renewing and a spiritual awakening among us!

Although praying is because of a relationship with God, we do expect results from our prayers. Ultimately we expect power and effectiveness from our praying. Perhaps you ask the question, "What does that look like?" or "What does that mean?" or "What can we expect from praying? While we can expect a closer walk with the Lord, we can also expect growth, intimacy, and results that come in the form of fire! Occasionally we should be instruments and witnesses of fresh encounters through prayer! There are some things God can do *(if we ask Him and trust Him)* that we have never seen Him do before.

God's presence brings life, joy, hope, peace, and love. God's presence showed up in the form of Jesus Christ in the New Testament. In Acts 2 on the Day of Pentecost, when 120 disciples were shut up in the upper room in a prayer meeting, God answered by fire! He is the God who answers by fire in the Old Testament, but He is also the God who answers by fire in the New Testament! Let us pray until the fire of God falls in times like these!

- Let the fire fall upon the congregation!
- Let the fire fall upon the preachers!

- Let the fire fall upon the choir!

- Let the fire fall upon the little children!

- Let the fire fall upon the young people!

- Let the fire fall upon the elderly!

- Let the fire fall upon the men!

- Let the fire fall upon the women!

- Let the fire fall upon the community!

- Let the fire fall upon the city!

- Let the fire fall upon the state!

- Let the fire fall upon the nation!

- Let the fire fall upon the world!

God is still setting people on fire! He is the God, who answers by fire, but He answers with prayer, He answers with power, and He answers with presence! May the people of God pray until He answers by fire! I know you may already know this, but you can trust the God who answers with fire. He's trustworthy, He's reliable, He's able, and He's capable. As we pray, may God answer by fire and let the fire fall!

Prayer:

O God you are "A Consuming Fire!" May Your power and presence fall upon us through the fire of the Holy Spirit as we pray. Lord so often we fall into the routine of rituals and habits without any passion for what you have called us to do. Lord, please return your fire to our prayers, our worship, the ministries, our marriages, our families, our congregations, and our communities. Lord, we pray in the Name of Jesus that You would let the fire fall! We pray that the fire will fall and deliver us from boredom, religious activity, sin, darkness, depression, doubt, division, disappointment, and discouragement. Lord, we need Your presence, power, protection, and your provisions. We can experience this when you answer our prayers by fire, In the Name of Jesus the Christ, we pray, Amen!

Questions for Discussion

1. Why is fire so important for our prayers?

2. What was so important about God answering by fire in Elijah's day? Why did Elijah need God to answer in this way?

3. What do you believe can hinder the fire of God from our prayers and our worship settings?

CHAPTER THIRTEEN

THANKSGIVING: OUR RESPONSE TO GOD'S GOODNESS!

O ne of the first phrases I was taught as a child was "thank you." It was important in our home that good manners were instilled into us and that we practiced it. It became a part of our family culture to say thank you when someone showed us an act of kindness. In our home you were scolded for not saying thank you when someone was nice to you. I have considered that the same measure should apply in the Kingdom of God. I wonder how God responds to us when we fail to give thanks to Him. My home training has helped me to be more grateful to God because He is always showing us acts of kindness. Lamentations 3:22-23 reminds us "It is of the Lord's mercies that we are not consumed,

His compassions fail not, they are new every morning, great is Thy faithfulness"(KJV). Now that's a pause for praise and thanksgiving on a daily basis! Per chance some are so engulfed in the troubles of life that we forget the triumphs of life. Then at other times we are so weighed down with the burdens that we can't realize the blessings. Yet, in the midst of troubles and blessings, we have something to thank God for! Thank you denotes appreciation and good manners. Thank you tells the giver that whatever was received, that gratitude is shown. Saying thank you is a common ground everyone can meet on. Thank you notes, letters, and cards are always in order because expressing thanks does not take the giver for granted.

Learning to pray prayers of thanksgiving is a good habit for the Christian. Just as it is important to appreciate others, it is of greater importance to show our gratefulness to God in response to His goodness! Therefore, just as we are appreciative to one another, we must use good manners with God. There are times when we pray not asking for anything but simply say, "Thank you, Lord!" As in adoration we offer a prayer of thanksgiving and praise for all that God does for us. Once a year we celebrate thanksgiving and gather with family and friends to tell God thank you. The question is, is that enough? With all God is to us and does for us, should not we thank Him more than once a year? Daily the Lord blesses us and teaches us to be thankful each day.

A number of years ago, our oldest son, Joshua who is a basketball fanatic and has been since before he was two years old, went to sleep with a ball in his hand. As he slept, the basketball rolled out of his hands. I went and picked up the ball, and as soon as I gave it to him his response was "thank you." I was elated that a two-year-old could remember without coercion the simple words "thank you" for a small kind act. I suppose it adds a greater understanding of what it means to our Heavenly Father when we tell Him thank you and show an attitude of gratitude towards Him. Surely, if a two-year-old can tell his daddy "thank you," we can tell God thank you! This is especially true when we consider what earthly parents do for their child is no comparison to all our Heavenly Father does for us.

Thanksgiving is a pause to praise and honor God for being at work in our lives. It also keeps us from having a pity party. Almost every day, we must encourage ourselves to find something to thank God for to keep us from complaining about what's not right. I believe that the saints can become so immune to the works of God that His blessings can become common place in our lives. We often hear it stated that God is still in the blessing business. If God is still in the blessing business, can we consider ourselves blessed when things don't go our way and find the heart to thank God anyway? Rather than resorting to fleshly motives and unthankful attitudes, a grateful heart will always honor God and bless us!

Could this have been the attitude of the one leprous man who returns in Luke 17 to thank Jesus for bestowing healing upon his life and ultimately upon his soul? During Biblical times those who had leprosy were declared unclean by the priest. They were isolated from the rest of society, including family and friends. When someone approached them, they had to make a startling announcement, saying, "Unclean, unclean!" But this day, as Jesus passed by, instead of crying out "unclean," they cried out, "mercy!" In an instant the healing power of Jesus Christ cured all ten of those lepers from their dreadful disease. Because Jesus understood the process, the priest had to declare them whole again. He commanded them to show themselves to the priest. In the process of going to the priest one of the lepers discovered a miracle and acknowledged his healing blessing and returned to appreciate the one who had blessed him. This is what praying a prayer of thanksgiving is all about: acknowledging the blessings and appreciating the blesser.

Acknowledge the Blessing

"When he saw he was healed..." (Luke 17: 15a., NIV). When the leper recognized that he had been healed, he turned back. He saw that he was no longer the same, and he acknowledged his healing. It's always important to be able to recognize a blessing when we see one. Sometimes we experience what many call "blessings in disguise," and the truth is we don't have to look very far to see the constant blessings of God in our lives. This was an answer to these lepers' prayers. They prayed for mercy and received it. As we pray and experience unusual answers to our prayers, whether it is healing, deliverance, provisions, peace, strength, calling, or an unexpected miracle, it's always in order to have an attitude of gratitude. It keeps us from being ingrates toward the kindness and mercies of God. Because we live in an ungrateful and greedy world, doing more, wanting more, and getting more, we can lose sight of the blessings of God. Being thankful helps us to appreciate the prayers that have already been answered, the doors already opened, and the miracles already realized, and the people already delivered! Once we realize how blessed we are, we get a different perspective on life in general. Therefore when we pray, we must always include a word of thanks for our blessings. At times it helps us to be specific and name the blessings that we have received. However, acknowledging the blessings gets us grounded and connected with the goodness of God.

Appreciate the Blesser

". . . turned back, and with a loud voice glorified God, and he fell down on his face at His feet, giving Him thanks: and he was a Samaritan" (Luke 17b-16, NIV). The one leper healed would dare not show himself to the priest until he had shown appreciation to the One who was responsible for his healing. So he turns back and with an attitude of worship and thanksgiving falls down on his knees at the feet of Jesus and says, "Thank you!" Here is a person who has a heart full of thanksgiving, and in submission he falls at the feet of Jesus, glorifies God, worships Him, and offer thanks for the healing that has taken place in his life. The scripture notes that he was a Samaritan. Here is one not considered a full-blooded Jew, but he returns to thank Him. He perhaps was the one least likely to acknowledge Jesus for what had taken place. Yet, we are often reminded that those we often expect to ignore God can sometimes be the very ones to lead the way in praise, worship, and thanksgiving. The one leper teaches us the power and importance of praising and thanking God. Being moved by his gratitude, Jesus asked, "Were not all ten cleansed? Where are the other nine? Was no one found to return and give praise to God except this foreigner?" (Luke 17:18-19, NIV). Jesus already knew how the ten should have responded, but only one came. The nine represent those who are ungrateful and may take God's grace, goodness, and generosity for granted. However, many of us have suffered from the same affliction on occasion. It's easy to get caught up in a cycle of expecting God to do more without thanking Him for what He has already done. Then he said to him, "Rise and go; your faith has made you well" (Luke 17:17-20). While the leper received physical healing in his body, going back to return thanks also gave him spiritual healing and wellness. This is a good lesson for God's people: no matter how bad things are in life, we can always find something to thank God for and be appreciative that things are as well as they are and not worse.

It appears that the nine did not appreciate Jesus as much as they appreciated their healing. Praying to show appreciation to God tells Him that we think more of the Giver than we do His gifts. Whatever God has done we ought to thank him. If we are thoughtful, we will be thankful. This prayer gives us an opportunity to praise God with our sacrifice of thanksgiving. It does show that we want more from God than just things and blessings: we want a relationship with Him!

So often we can have a long wish list of things we want God to do for us, yet our list of thanksgivings should be just as long as our list of supplications. As we pray the prayer of thanksgiving, it reminds us of how blessed we really are. It keeps us from murmuring and complaining about what we do not have or what seems not to be right. It helps us in our daily adventures of life to know that God has blessed us already for more than we will ever be able to repay Him or we deserve. Therefore, thanking God and showing appreciation with our love, life, and lips is a grand and marvelous thing in the presence of God. There are so many things we can pray to thank God for; the list goes on forever. Look around: it is evident that we have so much to thank God for, and He continues to bless us over and over and again! Each day we wake up is another opportunity to tell God thank you! May we never get too busy and so engulfed in our problems, pain, and pressures that we fail to see the goodness of the Lord among us!

The Psalmist admonishes us to thank God as he writes,

- "It's a good thing to give thanks unto the Lord and to sing praise unto Thy name, O most High...." Psalm 92:1 (KJV).
- "Enter into His gates with thanksgiving, and into His

courts with praise: be thankful unto Him, and bless His name." Psalm 100:4 (KJV).

- "Give thanks unto the Lord; call upon His name: make known His deeds among the people." Psalm 105:1 (KJV).

- "Praise ye the Lord. O give thanks unto the Lord; for He is good: for His mercy endureth forever." Psalm 106:1; 107:1 (KJV).

What an awesome God we serve and He is and is worthy of our praise, thanksgiving, and worship. The following is a thank you list and you may add to it in the days, weeks, months, and even years to come.

A Prayer of Thanksgiving

Dear Lord, thank you for your friendship, fellowship, and faithfulness. I truly appreciate you being around. You have done more for me than I will ever be able to do for you. I want to thank you for the things you have done for me _____ (*name the most recent or specific acts of kindness).* I thank You from the bottom of my heart for so many gifts, people, and things. Thank you for giving me life and that more abundantly. Thank you for looking out for me when I could not look out for myself. Thank you for sending your only son, Jesus Christ, to die for our sins and for protecting us with your power and the blood of Jesus Christ. I thank you that in You I live, and move, and have my being (Acts); I can never thank you enough for all that you have done. Thank you for loving me eternally, intentionally, unconditionally! Thank you for guiding me, helping me, healing me, and holding me in tough, tight, and trying times. Thank you for answering so many prayers, so many times, and in so many ways! Thank you for the power and presence of the Holy Spirit who brings fire, strength, breath, and renewal to life and ministry. Words are not adequate to express to You how grateful I am to You. I just want to say, from the bottom of my heart, thank You! Thank You! Thank You! Amen.

Study Questions:

1. Why do you think only one person returned to give thanks to Jesus?

2. Why is it important that we learn to be grateful to God?

3. What moved Jesus about the Samaritan returning to say thanks?

4. How do I relate to this story of the ten lepers in my own person life?

5. What are you thankful to God for?

Prayer Activity:

1. Spend a day thanking God. (Use the chart above if it is helpful).

2. Find things to thank God for.

3. Write God a thank you note and see how many things you can put in the note, and read/pray them back to God.

Praying To Appreciate God! Thanksgiving

Thank God For **Salvation**	Thank God For **Peace**	Thank God For **Love**
Thank God For **Life**	Thank God For **Strength**	Thank God For **Family**
Thank God For **Church Family**	Thank God For **Friends**	Thank God For **Deliverance**
Thank God For **Vision**	Thank God For **Wisdom**	Thank God For **Knowledge**
Thank God For **Ministry**	Thank God For **Pastors**	Thank God For **Jobs**
Thank God For **Shelter**	Thank God For **Food**	Thank God For **Clothing**
Thank God For **Transportation**	Thank God For **What He's Done**	Thank God For **What He's Not Done**
Thank God For **Good Days**	Thank God For **Bad Days**	Thank God For **Troubles**
Thank God For **Growth**	Thank God For **Stability**	Thank God For **Faith**
Thank God For **Jesus Christ**	Thank God For **The Holy Spirit**	Thank God For **Forgiveness**
Thank God For **Air**	Thank God For **Water**	Thank God For **Marriage**
Thank God For **Children**	Thank God For **Parents**	Thank God For **Teachers**
Thank God For **Prayer**	Thank God For **Fasting**	Thank God For **His Word**
	Below you may add to your list	

CHAPTER FOURTEEN

THE CONCLUSION

⟶⟶

*I*n order to pray on purpose, prayer must be intertwined through every phase of life. If we are going to grow into strong believers in the Christian faith, prayer must be a key factor toward this process. Praying on purpose helps us to fit God everywhere and in everything we do. Because prayer is a chief means for spiritual growth, we can pray anywhere, anytime, and about anything. Whether things are up or down, good or bad, when we are happy or sad, we can pray because God is always around and with us! All of life can be connected with God through prayer because God is present at all times. Age, circumstances, ministry, time, place, or space does not exempt anyone from being in constant communion with God.

We often make plans for vacation, meals, and meetings. We even make appointments to the doctor, dentist, barbershop, hairdressers, and so forth. If we are intentional about planning our day with temporal things, how much more important is it that we intentionally plan our day for prayer? If we put other things and other people on our agenda, why not put God on the agenda? After all, "He's only a prayer away!"

I recall a story shared with me by the Reverend Dr. Ocie M. Brown. She talked about her youngest son, Chris. She noted that Chris was at the breakfast table with the rest of the family, and she asked him to pray and thank the Lord for the food. Chris bowed his head, closed his eyes, and prayed silently. When he finished she said to Chris, "Chris, I thought I asked you to pray." Chris responded, "I did," at which she responded, "but I didn't hear you," and Chris replied, "But Mama, I wasn't talking to you; I was talking to God." What a profound sense of prayer from the heart of an innocent child. Could it be that often our hindrance to prayer is either talking too much to other people, or wanting to be heard by others, rather than being heard by the Lord? If we are going to be intentional about spiritual growth, then we must talk to God.

Praying on purpose keeps our prayer life real and relevant. When we are purposeful in our times of prayer, privately or publicly, we can seek God according to the situation we are presently in. Praying the scriptures will always keep us connected to the will of God. Learning to pray like Jesus and watching Jesus pray at every turn of His life and ministry encourages us to become praying disciples. As we have discussed various segments concerning prayer, the time has come that we do more than talk about prayer; the time has come to pray. Whether we are praying to adore God, confessing our sins, asking for help, praying for another, surrendering to God, praying and fasting, or just thanking God, it keeps us in the habit and practice of prayer. Praying on purpose keeps our relationship with God as the top priority! If we do not talk with God and if God does not talk with us, how can we be attuned to God's will?

As we pray, it is important to know that praying is more than just calling or saying words. When we pray, there should be fervency and power in our prayers. We need the power of the Holy Spirit to ignite us so that our prayers will have power and life. I recall one evening at home when my middle son, Caleb, asked me to pray for him so that he would not have any bad dreams. Just out of habit and without much energy or thought, I prayed for Caleb. A few minutes later, he got out of bed and came back into our bedroom and said, "Mama, can you pray for me so that I don't have bad dreams?" I responded, "Boy, I have already prayed for you." Caleb replied, "Yea, but that didn't work." For a moment his mother and I laughed, and then I thought, how many times do we pray haphazardly, without thinking or seeking God about how we should pray? The lesson I learned from a seven-year-old was when we pray, we must make sure that our prayers are working. The only way they can work is through Holy Spirit–filled and directed praying!

Prayer is the order of the day for every Christian disciple. When we pray, God will move. Bill Hybels writes, "When we work, we work, when we pray, God works."[8] When we learn to pray, all of life falls in place, no matter what the circumstance might be. When prayer is effective, it moves God and changes things and people.

Reading this book or any book on prayer does not mean that we are certified prayer warriors. There is always room for improvement in the area of prayer. While I believe that a consistent prayer life is the greatest need of the hour, it has also become the greatest challenge of the hour. There are always forces

---

[8] Hybels, 13.

competing and vying for our attention, especially to take us away from communing with God. Studying and learning about prayer does not imply that we know everything there is to know about God or prayer. We will be forever learning about prayer and the ways of God through God. Reading prayer books will not make us super spiritual saints or effective prayer warriors. However, these books are a means of grace that will open doors to prayer in our lives and stir us to be more intentional about growing spiritually through prayer. Therefore, "Let us come boldly."

Whatever our lot is in life, let us talk to God when things are difficult, dark, and devastating. Let us talk to God, and when life throws you a curve ball, talk to God! When it seems that you can't talk with anyone else or no one else will listen, talk to God. If you feel lonely and alone, talk to God! Psalm 34:15, teaches us that, "The eyes of the Lord are upon the righteous, and His ears are open to their cry." (KJV). Prayer is indeed talking with God, but also allowing God to talk back to our hearts and minds. In such case, prayer is more than a routine or ritual, but a time of intimacy and refreshment with the Lord. As we realize this, then we can commune regularly, effectively, and relationally with the Lord. God will give us power to pray without ceasing, with perseverance, purpose, and power.

Each day, I encourage our children as they leave home to be prayerful. One day I asked our youngest son, Elijah, "What does it mean to be prayerful?"

He responded, "It means to be full of prayer!" For me, it just meant to pray, to stay connected to God, but he added a greater insight for me in stating "to be full of prayer." As I thought about his statement, I came to the realization that his response sums up what I have been attempting to communicate in this book. We must be full of prayer, always ready, ever willing, and on purpose to connect with God and to connect others with God. May God grant us the grace, wisdom, knowledge, strength, and boldness to be full of prayer that we might pray on purpose. May He guide us in praying with confidence, compassion, courage, commitment, concern, and care! Let us cultivate the discipline of prayer in our lives and thus enjoy living daily in the wonderful and supernatural presence of God! When we do that, then we can say we are praying on purpose and growing up in the Lord Jesus Christ as a Spiritually Intentional Disciple! Amen!

Endorsements

There is a God-given and God-driven passion within this powerful man of God, Eric Leake. In this marvelous work, Dr. Leake so lovingly and compassionately admonishes the church that "On Purpose" prayer will cause our fire to burn so bright that the demons of hell will have to back away from us! He reminds us that prayer should exceed theory and become our daily lifestyle, thereby enabling us to daily say to the enemy, "Today we fight!"

Rev. J. R. Bridgeman, Presiding Elder, Chattanooga District, Pastor, Thompkin Chapel A.M.E. Zion Church

Chattanooga, TN

I have found the book *Praying on Purpose* by Eric Leake to be a blessing to me on many levels. I am certain that it will also bless you, regardless of where you find yourself on the prayer continuum. If you are a pastor or spiritual leader, it will serve you well. If you are a novice or beginner at prayer, it will help you too. There were many positive truths and helpful suggestions that we all should incorporate into our prayer lives. These would help us to live the life of spiritual power and purpose that Christ has ordained for us to live.

Pastor Anthony Collins, Pastor, House of Worship

Author, 100 Days of Inspiration

Oak Ridge, Tennessee

I have been blessed to have known the Reverend Dr. Eric Leake for a number of years. I can say unequivocally that he is indeed a man of God who truly believes in the Power of Prayer. He lives the life that he has written about in the powerful book *Praying on Purpose: Intentional Growth through Prayer.* I don't care how many books you already have on the subject of prayer: this book is a "must read." Dr. Leake, the masterful craftsman that he is, has so structured and outlined each chapter that the major points will stay with you as you prepare to build your own personal prayer life. After reading this book, I guarantee you will never be the same. You will receive direction, protection, and correction that will lead you to spiritual maturity in Christ. I highly endorse this book and highly recommend that you not only read this book but share it with others who need to know the real formula for success: an active prayer life that will happen if you continue to *Pray on Purpose*.

Bishop Michael Angelo Frencher, Sr.,

Eastern West Africa Episcopal District, A.M.E. Zion Church

Greensboro, North Carolina

Praying on Purpose: Intentional Growth through Prayer is a marvelous work that carefully details all prayer facets and how we are to focus in our hearts, mind, and soul. Dr. Leake very eloquently talks about all who should engage in the practice of prayer and the power of prayer. This book wonderfully gives us a blueprint on leading prayer-focused lives and how to talk with God and how to listen to God when he speaks to us. With prayerful reading, thoughtful writing and quiet study, our growth is more than intentional: it is inevitable.

Dr. Sandra Gadson, International President, Women's Home And Overseas Missionary Society A.M.E. Zion Church

Flossmoor, Illinois

I recommend *Praying On Purpose.* I believe this book is especially relevant as it relates to developing an intimate prayer life. We will use it to empower our local intercessory prayer ministry, who in turn will share this rare tool with disciples all over the world. "What prayer can't do, simply can't be done."

Rev. George M. Greene, Pastor-Teacher,

Christian Home United Church of Christ

Apex, North Carolina

Praying On Purpose: Intentional Growth Through Prayer has come to fruition after years of preparation and experience. God has used Reverend Dr. Eric L. Leake as his messenger, teacher, and leader of faithful believers in their need to realize prayer is not a powerless religious ritual. Dr. Leake has exemplified prayer as a powerful prayer warrior and minister. He has shown us that prayer really works. Reading this book will be a blessing to those seeking a more effective prayer life.

Bishop Roy A. Holmes,

Northeastern Episcopal District, A.M.E. Zion Church

Farmington, Connecticut

Dr. Eric Leake is an anointed teacher/preacher with a passion for encouraging and instructing the Body of Christ. In his book *Praying on Purpose,* he points out that prayer is the heart and soul of every successful relationship with God. He graciously brings to our attention that in order to *pray with purpose*, one must learn to persevere in his/her prayer life. We must learn to be intentional about "fighting the good fight of faith" through persevering prayer. Dr. Leake brings us a critical message: *God wants to revolutionize your prayer life and your walk with Him.* Don't settle for anything less.

Bishop Louis Hunter, Sr.,

Mid-Atlantic I Episcopal, A.M.E. Zion Church

Suwanee, Georgia

"This book has been written to encourage, equip, and empower people in prayer . . . ." Mission accomplished! The reminders offered by Dr. Leake are so rich, relevant, and so real. The case made is biblically based and the star witness—Jesus—sways the jury with His demonstrated life of prayer. *Praying on Purpose* stands the test and is free to do that for which it was ordained. Thanks to this work, directed and empowered by God, we have the mandate *to* pray (1 Th.5:17), a model *of* prayer (Jesus' example), and a manual *on* prayer. Believers are now more fully equipped for the perpetual battle for the souls and salvation of the people of God.

Bishop Nathaniel Jarrett, Jr., A.M.E. Zion Church, Retired, Ministerial Staff, Martin Temple A.M.E. Zion Church Chicago, Illinois

Praying on Purpose is revolutionary! It provides a framework to enhance the personal and spiritual journey of everyone who turns the pages. As you turn a page in this innovative masterpiece, pages will turn in your lives. This dynamic model will prove relevant as a life application guide. It is a tool that can be used to refine prayer from a personal level in our lives. It is absolutely life changing!

Dr. Maureen Jones, Prayer Warrior, Martin Temple A.M.E. Zion Church, Public Service Administrator, State of Illinois Chicago, Illinois

Praying on Purpose is a significant contribution to the wealth of resources offered to Christians seeking to live a more meaningful, worshipful, and purposeful life. Dr. Leake has given us a book that represents the journey to the sacred well that he has personally drawn from throughout the breadth and depth of his effective ministry as a public servant and a private devotee of Jesus Christ. As one of Dr. Leake's prayer partners for nearly twenty years, I have benefitted from the serious accord he has given to the discipline of prayer and the power with which he has entreated God to move on purpose for people in need of direction, healing, peace, provision, grace, encouragement, love, and hope. He has demonstrated that prayer is "always the first and last order of business" on his agenda. This volume serves as a divine guide to the kind of spiritual introspection necessary to counter the clamor and cacophony of sounds and sights that distract us from the pursuit of the most important relationship that matters: between our soul and our Savior. The world will now receive the gift of prayer that Dr. Leake has generously shared with his family, friends, church, and community throughout his entire ministry. Thank you, God, for the spiritual genius and sacred gift of your servant, Eric Leake.

Dr. Lester A. McCorn,

Pennsylvania Avenue A.M.E. Zion Church

Baltimore, Maryland

Prayer is the conversation with God that provides strength in the midst of the storms of life that we all face at one time or another. It is often difficult for laity to fully understand the importance of prayer in the life of a pastor. While pastors regularly pray for the members of their congregations during times of crises—in times of illness, death, despair, frustration, addiction, etc.—it is the private prayers of pastors that allow them to stand before the people of God and deliver the Word of God. In this powerful and personal text, Rev. Dr. Eric Leake offers a detailed guide for clergy and laity into a deeper relationship with God that reveals the inexhaustible source of strength. Dr. Leake's book cannot be fully appreciated in a single reading or in a single sitting. It requires careful contemplation and reflection. Leaders of congregations, both laity and clergy, will benefit enormously from Dr. Leake's contribution to the church through this book. It is a valuable resource for those who desire to equip God's people for the challenges that we face.

Rev. Dr. Jon E. McCoy, Senior Pastor,

St. Mark United Methodist Church

Chicago, Illinois

My friend Eric Leake has provided a challenging message to the church about the place of prayer in our lives. You will be challenged to refine your thinking about the beautiful practice of the Christian life through the pages of this book. Read it, wrestle with the Scriptures, and be encouraged to pray with boldness.

Dr. Philip Nation, Director, Adult Ministry Publishing, Life

Way Christian Resources, General Editor of

The Mission of God Study Bible and author of Compelled by Love

Nashville, Tennessee

Many people talk about prayer because they believe it is the right thing to do. Eric Leake is not one of those persons. I know him to be a man who believes in the power of prayer and demonstrates that through passionately and persistently calling others to do the same. *Praying on Purpose* reflects his commitment to equipping God's people to be more effectual in their prayer lives. It also reflects his unshakeable belief in the God to whom he is praying. Eric has searched the scriptures to give us sound biblical instruction on how to become who God desires us to be through the vital discipline of prayer.

Pastor Jason Perry, Pastor of Discipleship and Outreach,

Living Springs Community Church

Flossmoor, Illinois

Dr. Eric L. Leake has done a tremendous work in covering every aspect of prayer. Sound biblical teaching with practical application tools for those who are serious about connecting and dialoging with the Lord for victorious living.

Rev. Derrick Simmons, Pastor,

Daniel Chapel A.M.E. Zion Church

Phoenix, Illinois

I was blessed with the opportunity to review *Praying on Purpose: Intentional Growth through Prayer* prior to its initial publishing. I gained a renewed and lasting perspective on the importance and benefits of an effective and sustained prayer life. The information I gleaned from this book reaffirms that having knowledge or "knowing" is a good thing, but exercising wisdom (the application of knowledge) is more beneficial to achieving a fruitful and victorious Christian walk. It is essential for the Christian to possess the wisdom to couple prayer with biblically based fasting if they desire an intimate and obedient relationship with our Lord and Savior Jesus the Christ. Therefore; having powerful tools such as prayer and fasting and allowing them to lie dormant or go unused is akin to experiencing hunger and having a freezer full of food but willfully choosing not to open it up. The principles, practices, and processes detailed in this book are extremely powerful and if consistently exercised will bless you, too!

Mr. Anthony D. Smith, Partner in Prayer,

Greater Warner Tabernacle A.M.E. Zion Church

Knoxville, Tennessee

This book *Praying on Purpose* is awesome! The author has given a complete guide for prayer. He has preached on prayer, he has taught on prayer, and he is a praying man. The book is beautifully written.

Mrs. Mildred Summey, 6:00 AM Community Prayer Group

Knoxville, Tennessee

Why do so few people show up for prayer meetings or express interest in prayer? Could it be that people don't truly understand the power and benefits that are found in communing with God? As a result, Dr. Eric Leake is deeply involved with and committed to the ministry of prayer. Prayerfully, the information in this text will serve to encourage your hearts and minds to pray; 'praying always in the Spirit." May you become so engrossed in prayer that prayer will be as natural as breathing, eating, and sleeping.

Mrs. Helen Tolbert, Partner in Prayer,

Martin Temple A.M.E. Zion Church

Chicago, Illinois

It was the fall of 1991, my first year of Seminary, that one of my fellow classmates introduced me to a book titled *The Power of Prayer* by E.M. Bounds. Little did he know the profound impact that both he and the book would make upon my life. That person was Dr. Eric Leake, and once again he presents to me another book on prayer that, after reading it, has fanned the flames of devotion and driven me to my knees before God. Why another book on prayer you may ask? Because the times we are living in have grown increasingly decadent, the Church has become increasingly withdrawn from the altar of sacrificial prayer. Who better to redirect our focus back to the most important factor in building and developing a committed and consistent devotional life, than Dr. Leake? This is not just a book that has been written based solely on a scriptural understanding of prayer, but a book that is birthed from the heart of one who has intimate conversations with the Father. I am so proud and honored to not only endorse this book, but I highly recommend that you observe and follow the life of a true intercessor, man of God and friend.

Bishop Kenneth M. Yelverton, Senior Pastor,

The Temple of Refuge International Fellowship,

Author of *Sex and the Kingdom*

Charlotte, North Carolina

CPSIA information can be obtained
at www.ICGtesting.com
Printed in the USA
LVOW12s1945041017
551169LV00003B/555/P